AWS Certified Cloud Practitioner Exam Prep

500 Practice Questions

1ˢᵗ Edition

www.versatileread.com

Document Control

Proposal Name	:	AWS Certified Cloud Practitioner Exam Prep: 500 Practice Questions
Document Edition	:	1st
Document Release Date	:	14th June 2024
Reference	:	CLF-C02
VR Product Code	:	20242002CLFC02

Feedback:

If you have any comments regarding the quality of this book or otherwise alter it to better suit your needs, you can contact us through email at info@versatileread.com

Please make sure to include the book's title and ISBN in your message.

About the Contributors:

Nouman Ahmed Khan

AWS/Azure/GCP-Architect, CCDE, CCIEx5 (R&S, SP, Security, DC, Wireless), CISSP, CISA, CISM, CRISC, ISO27K-LA is a Solution Architect working with a global telecommunication provider. He works with enterprises, mega-projects, and service providers to help them select the best-fit technology solutions. He also works as a consultant to understand customer business processes and helps select an appropriate technology strategy to support business goals. He has more than eighteen years of experience working with global clients. One of his notable experiences was his tenure with a large managed security services provider, where he was responsible for managing the complete MSSP product portfolio. With his extensive knowledge and expertise in various areas of technology, including cloud computing, network infrastructure, security, and risk management, Nouman has become a trusted advisor for his clients.

Abubakar Saeed

Abubakar Saeed is a trailblazer in the realm of technology and innovation. With a rich professional journey spanning over twenty-nine years, Abubakar has seamlessly blended his expertise in engineering with his passion for transformative leadership. Starting humbly at the grassroots level, he has significantly contributed to pioneering the Internet in Pakistan and beyond. Abubakar's multifaceted experience encompasses managing, consulting, designing, and implementing projects, showcasing his versatility as a leader.

His exceptional skills shine in leading businesses, where he champions innovation and transformation. Abubakar stands as a testament to the power of visionary leadership, heading operations, solutions design, and integration. His emphasis on adhering to project timelines and exceeding customer expectations has set him apart as a great leader. With an unwavering commitment to adopting technology for operational simplicity and enhanced efficiency, Abubakar Saeed continues to inspire and drive change in the industry.

Dr. Fahad Abdali

Dr. Fahad Abdali is an esteemed leader with an outstanding twenty-year track record in managing diverse businesses. With a stellar educational background, including a bachelor's degree from the prestigious NED University of Engineers & Technology and a Ph.D. from the University of Karachi, Dr. Abdali epitomizes academic excellence and continuous professional growth.

Dr. Abdali's leadership journey is marked by his unwavering commitment to innovation and his astute understanding of industry dynamics. His ability to navigate intricate challenges has driven growth and nurtured organizational triumph. Driven by a passion for excellence, he stands as a beacon of inspiration within the business realm. With his remarkable leadership skills, Dr. Fahad Abdali continues to steer businesses toward unprecedented success, making him a true embodiment of a great leader.

Muniza Kamran

Muniza Kamran is a technical content developer in a professional field. She crafts clear and informative content that simplifies complex technical concepts for diverse audiences, with a passion for technology. Her expertise lies in Microsoft, cybersecurity, cloud security and emerging technologies, making her a valuable asset in the tech industry. Her dedication to quality and accuracy ensures that her writing empowers readers with valuable insights and knowledge. She has done certification in SQL database, database design, cloud solution architecture, and NDG Linux unhatched from CISCO.

Table of Contents

About AWS Certified Cloud Practitioner Exam

Introduction

Introducing the AWS Certified Cloud Practitioner (CCP) certification—a foundational milestone in the realm of AWS cloud computing. Tailored for individuals with limited or no prior experience in IT or cloud technologies, this certification offers a broad yet accessible overview of essential concepts, services, and terminology within the AWS ecosystem. Serving as a gateway to cloud-focused careers, the CCP certification provides the necessary foundational knowledge to navigate the AWS platform effectively. Whether you're a beginner in cloud computing, an IT professional seeking to broaden your skills, or a non-technical professional looking to enhance your cloud literacy, the AWS CCP certification sets the stage for success in the dynamic world of cloud computing.

What is AWS CCP?

The AWS Certified Cloud Practitioner certification is designed as an introductory step into the realm of AWS cloud computing, catering particularly to individuals with limited or no prior experience in IT or cloud technologies. It serves as a foundational milestone, offering a broad yet accessible overview of essential concepts, services, and terminology within the AWS ecosystem. By focusing on high-level understanding rather than technical intricacies, the certification ensures that beginners can grasp fundamental cloud computing principles without feeling overwhelmed by complex technical details. This makes it an ideal starting point for those looking to transition into a cloud-focused career, providing them with the necessary foundational knowledge to navigate the AWS platform effectively. Moreover, for non-technical professionals such as line-of-business employees, the certification offers a valuable opportunity to develop basic cloud literacy, enabling them to engage meaningfully with cloud-based systems and collaborate more effectively with technical teams. Ultimately, the AWS Certified Cloud Practitioner certification serves as a gateway for

6

individuals embarking on their journey into cloud computing, setting the stage for further learning and specialization in the AWS ecosystem.

Benefits of AWS CCP

The AWS Certified Cloud Practitioner (CCP) certification offers numerous benefits to individuals and organizations alike. For individuals, it provides a solid foundation in AWS cloud computing, covering essential services, concepts, and terminology. This foundational knowledge not only enhances career prospects but also boosts confidence in navigating the AWS ecosystem. With industry recognition and credibility, holding the AWS CCP certification validates one's expertise and commitment to cloud technologies, making them more appealing to employers seeking skilled cloud professionals.

Additionally, certified individuals gain access to a range of resources and opportunities within the AWS community, further supporting their professional growth and development. For organizations, having certified employees improves their cloud capabilities and competitiveness, ensuring teams possess a common understanding of cloud best practices and can effectively leverage AWS services. Ultimately, the AWS Certified Cloud Practitioner certification serves as a valuable asset for both individuals and organizations, empowering them to succeed in the dynamic world of cloud computing.

Prerequisites for the AWS CCP Exam

The AWS Certified Cloud Practitioner (CCP) exam doesn't have strict prerequisites in terms of required experience or previous certifications. However, candidates should have a basic understanding of cloud computing concepts and familiarity with AWS services.

The intended audience for the AWS CCP Certification Course?

The intended audience for the AWS Certified Cloud Practitioner (CCP) Certification Course encompasses a diverse range of individuals, including:

- **Beginners in Cloud Computing**: Those who are new to cloud computing and seeking to establish a foundational understanding of cloud concepts, services, and terminology.
- **IT Professionals**: Individuals working in IT roles who want to broaden their knowledge and skills in cloud computing, particularly within the AWS ecosystem.
- **Non-Technical Professionals**: Employees from non-technical backgrounds or roles such as sales, marketing, finance, or management who require a basic understanding of cloud computing to effectively collaborate with technical teams or understand the implications of cloud technologies on their work.
- **Students and Graduates:** Those pursuing education or recently graduated with degrees in computer science, information technology, or related fields who wish to kickstart their careers in cloud computing.
- **Career Switchers**: Individuals transitioning from other fields or industries into cloud computing careers who need to acquire fundamental cloud literacy and skills to enter the job market.
- **AWS Enthusiasts:** Hobbyists or enthusiasts interested in exploring AWS cloud services for personal projects or self-learning purposes.

The Certification Exam

The AWS Certified Cloud Practitioner (CCP) exam evaluates candidates' understanding of foundational AWS cloud concepts and services. Here's how it assesses their comprehension:

- **AWS Cloud Concepts:** Candidates are tested on their understanding of basic AWS cloud terminology, such as Regions, Availability Zones, and Edge Locations. They should grasp the fundamental concepts of cloud computing and how AWS provides scalable, reliable, and cost-effective solutions.
- **Core AWS Services:** The exam covers essential AWS services across various categories, including computing, storage, networking, databases, and security. Candidates should demonstrate familiarity with services like Amazon EC2, Amazon S3, Amazon RDS, Amazon VPC, AWS IAM, and others.

- **AWS Architecture and Infrastructure**: Candidates are evaluated on their knowledge of AWS global infrastructure, including Regions, Availability Zones, and Edge Locations. They should understand how these components are interconnected and how they contribute to AWS's high availability and fault tolerance.

- **AWS Security and Compliance:** The exam assesses candidates' understanding of AWS security best practices, compliance standards, and shared responsibility models. They should be able to identify security features and controls within AWS services and know how to implement security measures effectively.

- **AWS Pricing and Billing**: Candidates are tested on their knowledge of AWS pricing models, cost management practices, and tools for estimating and controlling costs. They should understand the factors that influence AWS pricing and be able to optimize costs for different use cases.

- **AWS Support Plans and Services:** The exam evaluates candidates' understanding of AWS support plans, service-level agreements (SLAs), and the different levels of AWS support. They should be familiar with the support options available and know how to access AWS support resources.

- **Cloud Deployment and Operations:** Candidates should demonstrate basic knowledge of cloud deployment and operational practices, such as provisioning resources, monitoring performance, and managing access control. They should understand how to deploy and operate AWS services securely and efficiently.

Exam Preparation

Before Exam

To prepare for the AWS Certified Cloud Practitioner (CCP) exam, it's crucial to begin by thoroughly reviewing the exam guide provided by Amazon Web Services (AWS). This guide outlines the domains and topics covered in the exam, giving you a clear roadmap of what to focus on. Once you've familiarized yourself with the content, it's time to dive into study materials. Utilize a variety of resources such as AWS whitepapers, official AWS documentation, online courses, and practice exams to reinforce your understanding of fundamental AWS concepts.

Day of Exam

Preparing for the AWS Certified Cloud Practitioner (CCP) exam requires careful planning and focus. On the day of the exam, arrive early at the testing center to complete check-in procedures smoothly. Remember to bring all necessary documents, including valid identification and any materials specified by the exam center.

During the exam, maintain a calm and concentrated mindset. Take deep breaths to manage any nervousness, and read each question carefully to grasp its requirements fully. Stay confident in your abilities and pace yourself to manage time effectively. If you encounter challenging questions, consider flagging them for later review if time allows.

After Exam

After completing the exam, take time to assess your performance. Identify strengths and areas for improvement. If possible, review missed questions to understand why you answered them incorrectly and learn from those mistakes. This reflective process enhances your understanding and readiness for future exams or real-world applications.

Exam Information

Prior Certification		Exam Validity	
Not Required		3 Years	
Exam Fee		Exam Duration	
$100 USD		90 Minutes	
No. of Questions		Passing Marks	
65 Questions		65-75%	

Recommended Experience
6 months exposure to the AWS cloud, Basic understanding of IT services and their uses in AWS cloud

Exam Format
Multiple Choice, Multiple Select

AWS CCP Exam Preparation Pointers

Preparing for the Azure AWS CCP certification exam requires a structured approach to ensure readiness and confidence on exam day. Here are some pointers specifically tailored for the AWS Certified Cloud Practitioner (CCP) exam:

1. **Understand AWS Fundamentals:** Ensure you have a solid understanding of basic AWS services, concepts, and the AWS global infrastructure. Topics such as AWS Regions, Availability Zones, and core services like EC2, S3, and IAM are essential.

2. **Review Exam Guide and Sample Questions:** Familiarize yourself with the exam guide provided by AWS, as it outlines the topics covered and the format of the exam. Practice with sample questions to get a feel for the types of questions you'll encounter.

3. **Hands-On Experience:** While not mandatory, hands-on experience with AWS services can significantly enhance your understanding and confidence. Consider using AWS Free Tier to experiment with different services.

4. **Study Resources:** Utilize various study resources such as official AWS documentation, whitepapers, online courses, and practice exams. AWS offers training courses specifically designed for the CCP exam.

5. **Focus on Security and Compliance:** Understand AWS security best practices, compliance standards, and how AWS implements security controls across its services. Topics like IAM policies, encryption, and the AWS Shared Responsibility Model are crucial.

6. **Cost Management:** Be familiar with AWS cost management practices, including pricing models, cost optimization techniques, and tools like AWS Cost Explorer. Understanding how to estimate and control costs is important for the CCP exam.

7. **Service Differentiators:** Understand the key features, use cases, and differentiators of various AWS services. This includes knowing when to use one service over another based on specific requirements or scenarios.

8. **Exam Strategy:** During the exam, carefully read each question and all answer choices. Eliminate obviously incorrect options to narrow down choices if you're unsure. Manage your time effectively to ensure you can answer all questions.

Job Opportunities with AWS CCP Certifications

The AWS Certified Cloud Practitioner (CCP) certification, similar to the AZ-900 for Microsoft Azure, lays a solid foundation for cloud computing knowledge, specifically within the Amazon Web Services (AWS) ecosystem. While it might not qualify you for highly technical roles, it can open doors to various entry-level and foundational positions in cloud computing, especially those focused on AWS. Here's a look at some potential career paths:

Entry-Level IT Roles:

- **Cloud Support Specialist:** Assisting users with basic AWS services and troubleshooting cloud-related issues.
- **Technical Support Specialist:** Providing technical support for applications or infrastructure deployed on AWS.

- **IT Help Desk Analyst:** Offering general IT support with a potential focus on resolving cloud-related inquiries.

Cloud Administration (Foundational Roles):

- **Junior Cloud Administrator:** Performing basic cloud administration tasks under supervision, such as user provisioning and resource management within the AWS platform.
- **Cloud Operations Associate:** Assisting with cloud deployments, monitoring AWS resources, and handling basic troubleshooting.

Other Potential Opportunities:

- **Cloud Sales Associate:** Leveraging your understanding of AWS fundamentals to explain cloud benefits and AWS services to potential customers.
- **Business Analyst:** Utilizing cloud knowledge to analyze business needs and identify potential solutions that can be implemented on AWS.
- **Project Coordinator (Cloud Focus):** Coordinating cloud-related projects, ensuring tasks align with AWS functionalities and best practices.

Demand for AWS CCP Certification in 2024

The demand for the AWS Certified Cloud Practitioner (CCP) certification is expected to remain strong in 2024 for several reasons:

- **Surging Cloud Adoption:** Cloud computing continues to experience explosive growth across all industries. As more companies migrate to the cloud, the need for professionals with a foundational understanding of AWS services will keep rising.
- **Entry Point to AWS Expertise:** The AWS CCP serves as the gateway to the world of AWS certifications. Earning this credential demonstrates a basic grasp of cloud concepts, AWS functionalities, and best practices. This makes it valuable for anyone interested in pursuing a career in cloud computing, particularly those focusing on AWS.

- **Validation of Basic Cloud Skills:** Even in non-technical roles, having the AWS CCP showcases a basic understanding of cloud computing, potentially giving you an edge in the job market. Employers increasingly value cloud literacy across various departments.

Practice Questions

1. What is the primary benefit of cloud computing in terms of cost?
A. It increases the capital cost of hardware and software.
B. It requires a large upfront investment in physical data centers.
C. It eliminates the capital expense of buying hardware and software.
D. It increases the need for in-house IT staff.

2. How does cloud computing contribute to a business's ability to scale globally?
A. By limiting the IT resources to local servers only.
B. By offering less computing power, storage, and bandwidth.
C. By providing IT resources with more or less computing power, storage, and bandwidth as needed.
D. By requiring businesses to predict their IT needs in advance.

3. Which of the following is an advantage of cloud computing in terms of speed and agility?
A. IT resources take a long time to become available.
B. IT resources are limited and cannot be scaled up.
C. IT resources are readily available for quick scaling.
D. IT resources require manual updates and patching.

4. What does the redundancy in cloud infrastructure imply?
A. There is no backup for hardware or software systems.
B. Critical components do not have backups in case of failure.
C. If one component fails, others are ready to take over.
D. Redundancy leads to increased downtime and inaccessibility.

5. How do cloud providers enhance the security of their services?
A. By avoiding the monitoring of their infrastructure.

B. By manually updating software once a year.

C. By constantly monitoring and proactively applying security patches.

D. By transferring all security responsibilities to the customer.

6. Which event does business continuity in cloud computing aim to address?

A. Regular system maintenance.

B. Predictable operational costs.

C. Unforeseen events like natural disasters or cyberattacks.

D. Routine data analysis tasks.

7. What does the shared responsibility model in cloud computing entail?

A. Cloud providers are solely responsible for all aspects of security.

B. Customers have no responsibility for their data and applications in the cloud.

C. Both cloud providers and customers work together to secure cloud resources.

D. Security is optional and can be customized by the user.

8. What aspect of cloud computing allows for continuous innovation?

A. The infrequent updates to services and features.

B. The constant innovation and introduction of new services by providers.

C. The requirement for users to purchase new hardware regularly.

D. The use of outdated technology to maintain compatibility.

9. Which cloud providers are considered the major players in the industry?

A. IBM, Oracle, and SAP.

B. Amazon, Google, and Azure.

C. Salesforce, VMware, and Red Hat.

D. HP, Cisco, and Alibaba Cloud.

10. According to the 2020 Centrify and CensusWide poll, what percentage of organizations had accelerated their cloud migration plans due to COVID-19?

A. 43%

B. 48%

C. 36%

D. 27%

11. Which economic foundation does cloud computing primarily rely on?

A. Fixed pricing

B. Subscription-based

C. Pay as you go

D. One-time purchase

12. What does CapEx stand for in cloud computing?

A. Current Expenditure

B. Capital Expenditure

C. Computing Expenditure

D. Cloud Expenditure

13. Which type of expenditure is cloud computing primarily associated with?

A. CapEx

B. OpEx

C. Non-recurring expenses

D. Fixed costs

14. What is the key benefit of cloud computing's consumption-based model?

A. High upfront expenses

B. Long-term asset ownership

VERSAtile Reads

C. Paying only for the resources used

D. Significant investment in infrastructure

15. What is the term for the capability to dynamically scale network resources in the cloud?
A. High Availability
B. Scalability
C. Elasticity
D. Agility

16. Which feature of cloud computing ensures zero downtime in the event of a fault?
A. Disaster Recovery
B. Fault Tolerance
C. Scalability
D. High Availability

17. What is AWS Lambda's pricing model based on?
A. Fixed monthly fees
B. The duration of resource retention
C. The execution of the function and resource usage
D. Number of virtual machines deployed

18. What is the main advantage of cloud computing in terms of resource deployment?
A. Manual configuration is required
B. The necessity to predict future resource requirements
C. Automatic deployment of resources at scale
D. Permanent allocation of resources

VERSAtile Reads

19. Which cloud computing service model allows businesses to use applications without managing the underlying infrastructure?
A. IaaS
B. PaaS
C. SaaS
D. DaaS

20. What kind of manageability allows for tracking resources' conditions and replacing failing ones automatically in the cloud?
A. Management of the Cloud
B. Management in the Cloud
C. Resource-based Management
D. Manual Management

21. Which cloud service model is responsible for managing the applications and services you deploy, while the cloud service provider typically manages everything else?
A. IaaS
B. SaaS
C. PaaS
D. Serverless

22. What does IaaS stand for, and what does it enable you to control?
A. Infrastructure as a Software; software applications
B. Infrastructure as a Service: virtual machine's operating system and networking attributes
C. Internet as a Service; network connectivity
D. Internet as a Software; web-based applications

23. Which of the following is NOT an advantage of using SaaS?
A. Global access from any internet-connected device

B. Easy access to cloud-based apps
C. Reduction in deployment time
D. Use of free client software

24. What is the main benefit of using a public cloud deployment model?
A. Exclusive computing resources
B. Lower costs due to scalability and flexibility
C. High-level data security and control
D. On-premises infrastructure

25. Which service model in cloud computing is closest to traditional on-premises software but is delivered over the internet?
A. IaaS
B. Serverless
C. PaaS
D. SaaS

26. Which deployment model allows for a shared infrastructure between multiple organizations?
A. Public Cloud
B. Private Cloud
C. Community Cloud
D. Hybrid Cloud

27. What is a significant benefit of the hybrid cloud model?
A. It offers the highest level of security and privacy.
B. It provides a flexible environment for legacy applications.
C. It is the most cost-effective model for all scenarios.
D. It allows dynamic workload balancing between private and public clouds.

28. What type of cloud service model typically includes handling software upgrades and security patches?
A. IaaS
B. PaaS
C. SaaS
D. Community Cloud

29. What is the main purpose of Amazon Web Services?
A. To provide gaming services
B. To offer cloud services, including computing power and database storage
C. To sell books and consumer goods online
D. To provide music streaming services

30. What does AWS Cloud Adoption Framework provide?
A. Legal advice for starting a new business
B. Guidance on operating enterprise systems on Amazon
C. A platform for social media marketing
D. Education on cloud computing for students

31. What feature of AWS allows businesses to easily adjust their computing resources?
A. Static scalability
B. Unmatched scalability
C. Limited flexibility
D. Manual scaling

32. What aspect of AWS helps ensure low latency and compliance with data residency laws?
A. Global infrastructure
B. Localized customer service

C. On-premises data centers

D. The use of third-party services

33. What is a key security feature of AWS?

A. Physical locks on data centers

B. Basic antivirus software

C. Identity and access control

D. Simple password protection

34. How does AWS address regulatory compliance for various industries?

A. By avoiding any data storage

B. Through a one-size-fits-all approach

C. By adhering to various compliance requirements

D. By outsourcing compliance to third parties

35. What does AWS's pay-as-you-go pricing model enable businesses and individuals to do?

A. Long-term fixed contracts

B. Flat-rate fees for all services

C. On-demand delivery of services with no cost control

D. On-demand delivery of services with cost flexibility

36. According to Andy Jassy, what do inventions require?

A. A strict business plan and high initial investment

B. The ability to try a lot of experiments and not having to live with the collateral damage of failed experiments

C. A large team and a physical storefront

D. Government subsidies and tax breaks

37. What is a major benefit of serverless services in AWS for startups?
A. They require large upfront investments
B. They can automatically scale with demand for little to no running cost
C. They need long-term commitment contracts
D. They are only suitable for large enterprises

38. What does AWS's virtual machine provisioning allow users to do?
A. Commit to a 3 to 5-year contract
B. Run a virtual machine indefinitely without costs
C. Terminate a virtual machine after a few minutes and only pay for the time it ran
D. Purchase hardware for their infrastructure needs

39. What should companies compare to decide their cloud migration strategy?
A. CapEx of different cloud providers
B. Benefits of operating each workload in the cloud versus on-premises
C. OpEx of different cloud services
D. The depreciation rates of their physical assets

40. How can maintenance of IT equipment be categorized in terms of expenditure?
A. Revenue Expenditure
B. Operational Expenditure (OpEx)
C. Capital Expenditure (CapEx)
D. Fixed Expenditure

41. Which AWS framework outlines six key principles for designing secure, reliable, efficient, and cost-optimized cloud architectures?
A. AWS Security Framework
B. AWS Operational Excellence Framework
C. AWS Well-Architected Framework

D. AWS Performance Framework

42. What is the primary benefit of automating infrastructure provisioning and configuration management on AWS?
A. Increases manual workload
B. Reduces consistency and speed
C. Reduces human error
D. Slows down deployments

43. How does AWS recommend protecting data in transit?
A. Use physical locks
B. Encrypt data
C. Store data offline
D. Use public networks

44. Which of the following is an AWS service that allows for the automatic scaling of resources?
A. Amazon RDS
B. AWS Lambda
C. Amazon S3
D. Amazon EC2 Auto Scaling

45. When designing your AWS architecture, why is it important to choose the right tools for the job?
A. To increase complexity
B. To optimize performance and costs
C. To use the most expensive services
D. To rely on a single service for all tasks

46. What is a cost-effective strategy to consider when using AWS?
A. Always use On-Demand Instances

B. Under-provision resources

C. Utilize Reserved Instances and Savings Plans

D. Ignore cost monitoring and tracking

47. Which AWS service is best suited for environmentally efficient operations due to lower energy consumption?

A. Amazon EC2

B. Amazon S3

C. AWS Lambda

D. Amazon DynamoDB

48. What is the benefit of having a stateless application in terms of scalability?

A. It can only scale vertically

B. It requires constant human intervention

C. It cannot service any request with available computing resources

D. It can easily scale horizontally

49. For which component of an application is Amazon RDS a scalable solution?

A. Stateless applications

B. Stateless components

C. Stateful components

D. Distributed processing

50. Which AWS service handles the distributed processing of large amounts of data?

A. Amazon EC2

B. Amazon S3

C. AWS Lambda

D. Amazon Elastic Map Reduce (EMR)

51. What is the primary benefit of treating servers as disposable resources in a cloud computing environment?

A. Increased hardware longevity

B. More physical server space

C. Quicker replacement and scalability

D. Reduced automation

52. What is bootstrapping in the context of the AWS cloud environment?

A. A method for securing data transmission

B. The process of executing scripts after launching a resource to enable reuse

C. The initial financial investment for cloud resources

D. Creating a default user interface for applications

53. What is a golden image in AWS?

A. A premium support plan

B. An award for excellent cloud architecture

C. A snapshot of a particular state of a resource used in auto-scaling

D. A physical backup of AWS data centers

54. What is the purpose of loose coupling in system architecture?

A. To increase the data transfer speed between components

B. To decrease the reliance of components on each other

C. To make the user interface more complex

D. To couple system components permanently

55. Which AWS service is used for creating, publishing, maintaining, and monitoring APIs?
A. AWS Lambda
B. Amazon EC2
C. Amazon API Gateway
D. Amazon S3

56. What is the function of Service Discovery in a loosely coupled architecture?
A. To provide detailed documentation for services
B. To allow services to find and communicate with each other
C. To increase the processing power of services
D. To serve as a backup for services

57. What is the benefit of using technology-specific interfaces such as RESTful APIs in system design?
A. They increase the dependency between components.
B. They allow for a graphical representation of data.
C. They allow teams to modify operations without affecting other components.
D. They are exclusively used for mobile applications

58. How does Amazon's Elastic Load Balancer contribute to a loosely coupled system?
A. By encrypting data at rest
B. By redirecting requests to a copy of the database in another availability zone if needed
C. By providing a physical backup location
D. By increasing the computational power of the system

59. What is the role of an Amazon SQS Queue in asynchronous integration?
A. To increase the speed of direct communication between components
B. To store messages for processing in case a component fails
C. To serve web content at low latency
D. To provide real-time data synchronization

60. What is a key practice when designing architectures using AWS?
A. Manually provisioning infrastructure across regions
B. Ignoring new AWS services and features to maintain stability
C. Consulting with AWS architects and partners for guidance
D. Focusing solely on technology without considering business goals

61. What is the main benefit of designing applications with graceful failure?
A. To ensure that applications never fail
B. To increase dependency between components
C. To handle component failure in a manner that minimizes impact on users
D. To ensure that applications use only managed services

62. What is one of the best design practices when developing large-scale applications on AWS?
A. To use as few services as possible for simplicity
B. To manage all server configurations manually
C. To leverage a broad set of AWS services
D. To rely solely on Amazon EC2 for all needs

63. Why should developers rely on AWS-managed services?
A. To increase the complexity of their applications
B. To make their applications harder to maintain

C. To reduce the need to manage server infrastructure

D. To ensure they are using servers instead of services

64. What is Amazon S3 particularly good for, according to exam tips?

A. Dynamic web hosting

B. Static website hosting

C. Real-time analytics

D. Complex database management

65. What type of architecture does AWS Lambda support?

A. Monolithic

B. Server-heavy

C. Serverless

D. Tight coupling

66. Which AWS service would you use for customizable architecture with full control?

A. Amazon S3

B. Amazon API Gateway

C. AWS Lambda

D. Amazon EC2

67. What does tight coupling in a system signify?

A. Independence between hardware and software components

B. Minimal interaction between systems and applications

C. A high degree of interdependence between components

D. The use of AWS-managed services

68. What is the potential downside of a tightly coupled system like a bank ATM?

A. It can operate independently without any external systems.

B. It is easy to make changes to one component without affecting others.

C. If one component fails, it may cause the entire system to fail.

D. It relies heavily on serverless architecture.

69. Which statement best describes monolithic applications?

A. They consist of loosely coupled, small, independent components.

B. They have a single, large codebase with tightly coupled functionalities.

C. They are primarily built using serverless architectures.

D. They function without any interdependencies between their components.

70. What are the two types of partners in the AWS Partners Program?

A. Performance partners and Auditing partners

B. Consulting partners and Technology partners

C. Service Control Policy partners and IAM Policy partners

D. Quick Start partners and CloudFormation partners

71. What is the primary benefit of using a microservices architecture over a monolithic model?

A. Microservices are always written in Java.

B. Microservices require more operational overhead.

C. Microservices are more difficult to deploy.

D. Microservices allow for independent deployment of loosely connected services

72. How do microservices typically communicate with each other?

A. Through shared databases

B. Via APIs

C. By email

D. Through FTP transfers

73. What are the six pillars of the AWS Well-Architected Framework?

A. Design, Build, Deploy, Monitor, Scale, and Document

B. Operational Excellence, Performance, Compatibility, Security, Cost, and Support

C. Operational Excellence, Security, Reliability, Performance Efficiency, Cost Optimization, and Sustainability

D. Infrastructure, Software, Platform, Data, Analytics, and Machine Learning

74. What is the purpose of the AWS Well-Architected Tool?

A. To provide gaming services

B. To automate software development

C. To facilitate cloud infrastructure assessment and improvement tracking

D. To offer legal advice on cloud compliance

75. What aspect of cloud workloads does the sustainability pillar of the AWS Well-Architected Framework address?

A. Profitability

B. Environmental impact

C. Code sustainability

D. Workload automation

76. What does an AWS Region consist of?

A. A single data center

B. Multiple isolated locations known as availability zones

C. An area with a centralized IT management

D. Several interconnected networks

77. What is the primary focus of the reliability pillar in the AWS Well-Architected Framework?
A. To ensure the lowest possible cost
B. To make sure workloads fulfill their intended functions
C. To maximize the speed of the application
D. To focus on the user interface design

78. How does the AWS Well-Architected Tool support collaboration?
A. By allowing users to play collaborative games
B. By providing shared music playlists
C. By enabling documentation and sharing of architecture with teams
D. By offering a chat system

79. What does loose coupling in a microservices architecture imply?
A. Services cannot communicate with each other.
B. Services are highly dependent on each other.
C. Services are connected but not dependent on each other.
D. Services require a monolithic infrastructure.

80. Which AWS Well-Architected Framework pillar focuses on allocating IT and computing resources efficiently?
A. Security
B. Performance Efficiency
C. Reliability
D. Cost Optimization

81. What is the purpose of an Availability Zone in AWS?
A. To host websites for businesses
B. To provide a collection of edge locations
C. To reduce the chance of simultaneous zone failures
D. To act as a CDN for AWS services

82. What are Edge Locations in AWS used for?

A. To store user data permanently

B. To cache data and reduce latency for end-user access

C. To provide a backup for Availability Zones

D. To host the main AWS infrastructure

83. How many Edge Locations does AWS currently have?

A. Less than 50

B. More than 102

C. Exactly 81

D. Over 200

84. What is the function of a Regional Edge Cache in AWS?

A. To replace the need for Availability Zones

B. To store static IP addresses

C. To retain expired data and serve cache misses from edge locations

D. To act as the primary data storage for AWS services

85. What is the AWS Global Accelerator primarily used for?

A. To manage AWS infrastructure

B. To improve the performance and availability of applications for users globally

C. To create new AWS regions

D. To replace traditional CDN services

86 What are the endpoints for a standard accelerator in AWS Global Accelerator?

A. Elastic IPs and Amazon EC2 Instances

B. Application Load Balancers and Network Load Balancers

C. Both A and B
D. Regional Edge Caches

87. How does AWS Global Accelerator enhance internet user performance?
A. By reducing the number of edge locations
B. By increasing the data storage capacity
C. By routing traffic through the Amazon backbone network
D. By eliminating the need for static IP addresses

88. What is the significance of the static IP addresses provided by AWS Global Accelerator?
A. They serve as a single fixed entry point for clients
B. They are used for internal AWS services only
C. They act as a backup for Regional Edge Caches
D. They are temporary and change frequently

89. What does AWS's Global Infrastructure not include?
A. 25 geographic regions
B. 81 availability zones
C. Over 100 edge locations
D. Dedicated physical stores for consumers

90. What is BYOIP in the context of AWS Global Accelerator?
A. Bring Your Own Internet Provider
B. Bring Your Own IP address range
C. Buy Your Own Internet Package
D. Backup Your Own Infrastructure Plan

91. What is the purpose of AWS Outposts?
A. To host web applications

B. To provide a platform for gaming

C. To extend AWS's infrastructure to on-premises facilities

D. To offer a new messaging service

92. Which of the following AWS services can be accessed locally through AWS Outposts?

A. EC2, EBS, ECS, RDS

B. Amazon Alexa, Amazon Kindle, Amazon Prime

C. AWS Lambda, AWS Lex, AWS Polly

D. Amazon Chime, Amazon WorkMail, Amazon WorkDocs

93. What are AWS Local Zones primarily used for?

A. To store data in different geographic locations

B. To provide low latency services in specific geographic areas

C. To offer discounted AWS services

D. To serve as data backup centers

94. How does AWS Wavelength cater to 5G-enabled applications?

A. By offering free 5G network subscriptions

B. By integrating AWS services directly into telecom providers' data centers

C. By providing a new 5G-enabled smartphone

D. By broadcasting 5G signals

95. What is the AWS Systems Manager used for?

A. Managing and troubleshooting AWS resources

B. Conducting online AWS certification exams

C. Managing Amazon retail operations

D. Providing customer support for AWS products

96. Which of the following is NOT a feature of AWS Systems Manager?
A. Patch management
B. Session management
C. Automated resource grouping
D. Web hosting

97. What is the role of SSM Agent in AWS Systems Manager?
A. It processes payments for AWS services
B. It manages user access and permissions
C. It performs configuration changes and operations on resources
D. It serves as a virtual assistant for AWS users

98. Which AWS service is suitable for applications requiring extremely low latency, like real-time analytics?
A. AWS Outposts
B. AWS Wavelength
C. AWS Local Zones
D. AWS Direct Connect

99. Which AWS solution supports edge computing scenarios by bringing AWS services closer to end-users or devices?
A. AWS Outposts
B. AWS Local Zones
C. AWS Wavelength
D. All of the above

100. What is a managed node in the context of AWS Systems Manager?
A. A network switch managed by AWS
B. A user account with administrative access

C. A computing resource like an EC2 instance or on-premises server

D. A storage device like Amazon S3

101. What is the maximum size of an object that can be stored in an Amazon S3 bucket?

A. 1 TB

B. 5 TB

C. 10 TB

D. 50 TB

102. Amazon S3 buckets are unique and can be accessed globally. How are they identified?

A. By a unique version ID

B. By a globally unique name

C. By the region they are created in

D. By the key associated with each object

103. Which AWS service is designed for object storage with a simple web service interface?

A. Amazon EC2

B. Amazon RDS

C. Amazon S3

D. Amazon EBS

104. What is the default privacy setting for a new Amazon S3 bucket?

A. Public Read Access

B. Public Write Access

C. Private with no public access

D. Public Read and Write Access

105. Which of the following is NOT a feature of Amazon S3?
A. Hosting dynamic websites with database connections
B. Scalable storage
C. Data transfer over SSL
D. High durability across multiple facilities

106. What does the key of an object in an S3 bucket represent?
A. The encryption type
B. The storage class
C. The unique identifier for the object
D. The metadata of the object

107. How can you optimize latency and minimize costs when creating an Amazon S3 bucket?
A. By setting a bucket policy for public access
B. By choosing an AWS Region close to your location
C. By using a unique bucket name
D. By limiting the number of objects in the bucket

108. What is the availability guarantee for objects stored using Amazon S3 Standard?
A. 99.9% availability
B. 99.99% availability
C. 99.999% availability
D. 100% availability

109. Which of the following options allows for concurrent read and write access to data in Amazon S3?
A. Bucket policies
B. Object metadata

C. Version ID

D. Scalability of storage

110. What can be used in Amazon S3 to manage object permissions?

A. SSL certificates

B. Version IDs

C. Bucket policies and access control lists (ACLs)

D. Metadata tags

111. Which storage class in Amazon S3 is designed for non-critical, reproducible data that can be stored with less redundancy than the standard storage class?

A. S3 Standard

B. S3 Standard-IA

C. S3 One Zone-IA

D. Reduced Redundancy Storage

112. Which Amazon S3 feature allows automatic replication of one bucket's contents to another bucket in a different AWS Region?

A. Cross-Region Replication

B. Lifecycle Management

C. Transfer Acceleration

D. Versioning

113. Upon successfully uploading a file to an S3 bucket, what HTTP status code is expected to be returned?

A. HTTP 202

B. HTTP 404

C. HTTP 200

D. HTTP 500

114. What consistency model does Amazon S3 provide for PUTS of new objects?
A. Consistent
B. Read after Write consistency
C. Eventual consistency
D. Strong consistency

115. Which Amazon S3 storage class is ideal for data that is accessed infrequently but requires rapid access when needed?
A. S3 Standard
B. S3 Standard-IA
C. S3 One Zone-IA
D. Reduced Redundancy Storage

116. What is the minimum object size for S3 Standard-IA and S3 One Zone-IA storage classes?
A. No minimum
B. 128 KB
C. 30 KB
D. 64 KB

117. Which S3 feature is used to share objects with URLs that are only valid for a specified and limited period?
A. IAM Policies
B. Bucket Policies
C. Query String Authentication
D. Access Control Lists (ACLs)

118. Which feature of Amazon S3 allows you to manage data access at scale for shared datasets in S3?
A. Bucket Policies
B. Access Points
C. IAM Policies
D. Access Control Lists (ACLs)

119. Which AWS service allows for centralized and automated backup across AWS services both in the cloud and on-premises?
A. Amazon Glacier
B. AWS Storage Gateway
C. Amazon S3
D. AWS Backup

120. What is the term used synonymously with 'backup' in AWS services?
A. Snapshot
B. Recovery Point
C. Archive
D. Object

121. Where does AWS Backup store its recovery points?
A. S3 Buckets
B. EC2 Instances
C. Backup Vaults
D. Glacier Vaults

122. Which Amazon service is optimized for infrequently accessed data and is ideal for long-term archiving and backup?
A. AWS Storage Gateway
B. Amazon EBS

C. Amazon S3
D. Amazon Glacier

123. What is the typical retrieval time for data stored in Amazon Glacier?
A. A few milliseconds
B. 3 to 5 hours
C. 3 to 5 minutes
D. Instant

124. Which AWS service is a downloadable virtual machine that connects on-premises software appliances with cloud-based storage?
A. Amazon S3
B. AWS Direct Connect
C. Amazon Glacier
D. AWS Storage Gateway

125. What feature of Amazon Glacier enforces compliance with a lockable policy?
A. SSL Encryption
B. Vault Lock
C. Lifecycle Management
D. Data Integrity Checks

126. How does AWS Backup help with regulatory compliance?
A. By providing instant data retrieval
B. By offering the lowest storage costs
C. By allowing centralized management of data protection policies
D. By using a downloadable virtual machine

127. What is the minimum storage duration for data in Amazon Glacier?
A. 30 days

B. 60 days

C. 90 days

D. 120 days

128. What is the maximum size supported for each volume in Volume Gateway Stored Mode?

A. 32TB

B. 16TB

C. 512TB

D. 1PB

129. How many volumes can a single gateway support in Volume Gateway Cached Mode?

A. 16 volumes

B. 32 volumes

C. 512 volumes

D. 1PB volumes

130. What is the maximum storage capacity per gateway in Volume Gateway Cached Mode?

A. 512TB

B. 1TB

C. 1PB

D. 16TB

131. What type of database would you opt for if you need to work with complex transactions and JOIN operations?

A. Amazon DynamoDB

B. Amazon Redshift

C. Amazon DocumentDB

D. Amazon Aurora

132. Which AWS service is a non-relational database that automatically scales horizontally?
A. Amazon RDS
B. Amazon DynamoDB
C. Amazon Aurora
D. Amazon Redshift

133. What is an AWS service that is specialized for the analysis and reporting of large amounts of data?
A. Amazon RDS
B. Amazon DynamoDB
C. Amazon DocumentDB
D. Amazon Redshift

134. Which AWS search service offers an open-source API and more control over configuration details?
A. Amazon CloudSearch
B. Amazon ES
C. Amazon RDS
D. Amazon DynamoDB

135. How does Amazon Neptune ensure high availability?
A. By deploying in a single Availability Zone
B. By synchronously replicating data across three Availability Zones
C. By using sharding
D. By employing standby mode for replicas

136. What kind of database is Amazon Neptune?
A. Relational Database

B. Key-Value Store
C. Graph Database
D. Data Warehouse

137. Which AWS service provides a managed in-memory cache to improve application performance?
A. Amazon ES
B. Amazon DynamoDB
C. Amazon ElastiCache
D. Amazon DocumentDB

138. What is the purpose of Amazon RDS Multi-AZ deployments?
A. To provide a data warehousing solution
B. To run complex queries
C. To automatically handle failover in case of an outage
D. To support NoSQL data models

139. What feature does Amazon DynamoDB offer for managing the lifecycle of items?
A. Multi-AZ deployments
B. On-demand backups
C. Time-to-live (TTL) settings
D. Horizontal scaling

140. Which of the following is a benefit of using AWS-managed services like Amazon RDS and Amazon DynamoDB?
A. They require extensive management of hardware and software configurations
B. They offer manual scaling options only
C. They handle routine database tasks such as provisioning, patching, and

backups
D. They do not offer automated backups

141. What is the main purpose of Amazon FSx for Windows File Server?
A. To provide a Linux-based file system
B. To offer a fully managed native Microsoft Windows file system for AWS
C. To optimize for compute-intensive workloads
D. To facilitate data transport and edge computing

142. Which AWS service cannot be connected to an EC2 instance running Windows?
A. Amazon FSx for Windows
B. Amazon FSx for Lustre
C. AWS Snowcone
D. Elastic File System (EFS)

143. Amazon FSx for Lustre is optimized for which kind of workloads?
A. Low-performance computing
B. File transport and edge computing
C. Standard web hosting
D. Compute-intensive workloads

144. What is the key difference between EFS and Amazon FSx for Windows in terms of application compatibility?
A. EFS is for SharePoint and IIS Web Server
B. EFS is compatible with Microsoft SQL Server
C. Amazon FSx for Windows is for Linux-based applications
D. Amazon FSx for Windows is for Windows-based applications

145. Which AWS service allows you to perform non-disruptive tests to ensure that disaster recovery implementation is finished?
A. AWS Snowcone
B. Amazon FSx for Windows
C. Amazon FSx for Lustre
D. AWS Elastic Disaster Recovery (AWS DRS)

146. What is the main use case for AWS Snowcone?
A. To provide a Windows-based file system
B. To optimize for machine learning models
C. For data transport and edge computing
D. To serve as a high-performance database server

147. Which version of AWS Snowcone offers SSD-based storage?
A. Snowcone with 8 TB of HDD-based storage
B. Snowcone with 2 vCPUs and 4 GB of memory
C. Snowcone SSD with 14 TB of SSD-based storage
D. Snowcone with NFS capability

148. Which AWS service can store data directly to Amazon S3?
A. Amazon FSx for Windows
B. AWS Elastic Disaster Recovery
C. Amazon FSx for Lustre
D. AWS Snowcone

149. How long can a Snowcone device operate on battery power with a light workload?
A. Approximately 2 hours
B. Up to about 6 hours
C. Around 12 hours
D. Nearly 24 hours

150. Which file interface do Snowcone devices provide?
A. Server Message Block (SMB)
B. Network File System (NFS)
C. Storage Area Network (SAN)
D. File Transfer Protocol (FTP)

151. What is the primary purpose of AWS Identity and Access Management (IAM)?
A. To manage AWS billing and subscription services
B. To launch and manage Amazon EC2 instances
C. To provide secured control access to AWS resources
D. To store data in the AWS Cloud

152. What is the recommendation regarding the use of the AWS account root user?
A. Use it for everyday access
B. Share it with trusted employees
C. Use it to create other IAM user accounts and secure it with multi-factor authentication
D. Use it for deploying applications

153. What can an IAM User represent?
A. Only a person within an organization
B. Only EC2 instances
C. A person, system, or application
D. Only AWS services

154. What is an IAM Group?
A. A collection of EC2 instances

B. A collection of IAM roles

C. A collection of IAM users

D. A collection of AWS accounts

155. What are the benefits of using IAM Roles over IAM Users?

A. IAM Roles provide permanent long-term credentials

B. IAM Roles can be used to directly interact with AWS services

C. IAM Roles offer temporary security credentials and are more secure

D. IAM Roles are used to manage billing services

156. Which of the following statements is true about IAM resources?

A. IAM resources are region-specific

B. IAM resources can only be managed through the AWS Management Console

C. IAM resources are global and can be used across regions

D. IAM roles can be attached to multiple instances

157. What is the default permission state for a new IAM user, group, or role?

A. Read-only access to all AWS services

B. Full administrative access

C. No permissions

D. Limited access to Amazon EC2

158. How can IAM policies be applied to an identity or resource?

A. By attaching a managed policy only

B. By adding a user to a group with no permissions

C. By cloning the instance profile of an EC2 instance

D. By attaching a managed policy, attaching an inline policy, or adding the user to a group with permissions

159. What is NOT a feature of IAM Groups?
A. A group can contain multiple IAM users
B. Groups can be nested within other groups
C. Groups can be used to manage permissions for a collection of users
D. A user can belong to multiple groups

160. Which IAM entity is used to delegate access within or between AWS accounts?
A. IAM Group
B. IAM User
C. IAM Role
D. IAM Policy

161. What is the primary purpose of a VPC endpoint in AWS?
A. To allocate public IP addresses to instances
B. To connect VPC to privately supported AWS services without requiring an internet gateway
C. To establish a VPN connection between remote networks and VPCs
D. To provide a connection to the internet for instances within a VPC

162. Which of the following are the two types of VPC endpoints in AWS?
A. Public endpoints and Private endpoints
B. Internet endpoints and Intranet endpoints
C. Interface endpoints and Gateway endpoints
D. Direct Connect endpoints and VPN endpoints

163. Which AWS service is supported by a Gateway Endpoint?
A. AWS Lambda
B. Amazon S3

C. AWS Elastic Beanstalk

D. Amazon EC2

164. What does an Interface Endpoint in a VPC use to secure traffic to services?

A. Prefix lists

B. Internet gateways

C. Security groups

D. NAT devices

165. What is AWS PrivateLink used for in the context of VPC endpoints?

A. To provide a direct connection to the internet

B. To enable public IP addresses for instances

C. To access AWS services privately using private IP addresses

D. To manage cross-region VPC peering

166. Which of the following is a limitation of VPC peering?

A. It supports transitive peering

B. It cannot be established between VPCs with overlapping CIDR blocks

C. It allows for more than one peering connection between the same two VPCs

D. It does not use the existing infrastructure of the VPCs

167. What is the main benefit of using an AWS Managed VPN?

A. It offers the highest bandwidth for data transfer

B. It provides a secure, tunneled connection over the internet

C. It avoids the need for any encryption protocol

D. It does not depend on an internet connection

168. Which AWS service enables logical connections from a remote network to Amazon VPC with potential bandwidth cost reduction?
A. AWS Direct Connect
B. AWS Managed VPN
C. Software VPN
D. AWS VPN CloudHub

169. What kind of routing decisions does an Application Load Balancer make?
A. Network Layer
B. Transport Layer
C. Application Layer
D. Data Link Layer

170. When would you use a Classic Load Balancer instead of the other types of ELB?
A. When you need to balance loads across multiple EC2 instances in EC2-Classic or a VPC
B. When you require advanced routing capabilities
C. When you need to handle volatile traffic patterns and low latencies
D. When you require TLS termination

171. What is the primary benefit of enabling Multi-Factor Authentication (MFA) for AWS accounts?
A. To increase the storage capacity of an AWS account
B. To add a layer of security to the username and password
C. To reduce the cost of AWS services
D. To improve the user interface of the AWS Management Console

172. Which of the following is NOT a supported MFA method on AWS?
A. U2F Security Key

VERSAtile Reads

B. Hardware MFA device

C. Virtual MFA Devices

D. SMS-based verification

173. What are IAM users required to submit when accessing AWS websites or services with MFA enabled?

A. A user ID

B. A security question answer

C. Unique authentication from an AWS-supported MFA method

D. A retinal scan

174. When using a virtual MFA device, what type of code must users provide during sign-in?

A. A four-digit numeric code

B. A ten-digit alphanumeric code

C. A six-digit numeric code

D. A unique word-based passphrase

175. What is the main difference between a U2F Security Key and a Hardware MFA device in terms of user interaction during sign-in?

A. A U2F Security Key requires a fingerprint scan, while a Hardware MFA device does not.

B. A U2F Security Key requires the user to manually input a code, while a Hardware MFA device requires a touch.

C. A U2F Security Key requires the user to touch the device, while a Hardware MFA device requires a code to be manually entered.

D. There is no difference; both require a USB connection.

176. What is the maximum number of authenticator apps that any individual user can have registered on AWS SSO MFA?

A. One

B. Two

C. Three

D. Four

177. Which of the following devices can serve as a Built-In Authenticator for WebAuthn?

A. TouchID on a MacBook

B. A traditional keyboard

C. A standard monitor

D. An external hard drive

178. How do FIDO2 and WebAuthn protect user privacy?

A. By erasing all user data after each session

B. By ensuring cryptographic data is unique across sites and biometric data never leaves the device

C. By using a common password for all sites

D. By encrypting data with a single-use key

179. What should users do if they encounter compatibility issues with U2F devices?

A. Immediately dispose of the device

B. Contact the U2F device provider

C. Ignore the problem and use a password-only login

D. Switch to using virtual MFA devices only

180. Which third-party authenticator applications can users utilize as an approved MFA device on AWS?

A. Those that support RFC 6238

B. Any SMS-based verification app

C. Apps that provide permanent codes

D. Apps that require physical mail verification

181. What is the primary service that Amazon CloudFront provides?
A. Web hosting
B. Data analytics
C. Content Delivery Network (CDN)
D. Database Management

182. Which of the following is NOT an origin type that can be used with Amazon CloudFront?
A. Amazon S3 bucket
B. Elastic Load Balancer
C. Amazon DynamoDB
D. HTTP server

183. What are the benefits of Amazon CloudFront's regional edge caches?
A. They provide unlimited storage for static content.
B. They help keep content closer to viewers for longer periods.
C. They replace the need for global edge locations.
D. They act as the primary storage for dynamic content

184. How does Amazon CloudFront deliver content to the user?
A. By always requesting content from the origin server.
B. By delivering content from the closest data center.
C. By routing the request to the edge location with the lowest latency.
D. By storing all content in the central Amazon S3 bucket.

185. What is the distribution in the context of Amazon CloudFront?
A. A single storage location for content before distribution
B. The collection of configuration and settings for a CDN

C. The name given to the CDN, consisting of a collection of edge locations

D. The process of delivering content to the end-users

186. What AWS service is seamlessly integrated with Amazon CloudFront to protect applications from threats?

A. AWS Inspector

B. AWS WAF

C. AWS GuardDuty

D. AWS IAM

187. Which feature allows you to run code across AWS locations worldwide in response to end-user actions?

A. AWS@Lambda

B. AWS Elastic Beanstalk

C. Lambda@Edge

D. AWS EC2 Instances

188. What is a key performance benefit of Amazon CloudFront?

A. Unlimited storage capacity

B. Direct connections with end-user ISPs

C. Free domain registration

D. Automatic code deployment

189. What is the pricing structure of Amazon CloudFront?

A. Fixed monthly subscription fee

B. One-time setup fee

C. Pay-as-you-go with minimum monthly commitments

D. Pay-as-you-go with no long-term contracts or minimum monthly usage commitments

190. Which AWS service does Amazon CloudFront not have a deep integration with?
A. Amazon S3
B. Amazon EC2
C. Elastic Load Balancing
D. Amazon RDS

191. What is the primary service provided by Amazon Route 53?
A. Web hosting
B. Database management
C. Cloud DNS web service
D. Content delivery network

192. What is the function of DNS in the context of Amazon Route 53?
A. To balance the load across servers
B. To encrypt web traffic
C. To distribute software updates
D. To translate domain names to IP addresses

193. Which of the following routing types is NOT supported by Amazon Route 53?
A. Latency-based routing
B. Geo DNS
C. Weighted round-robin
D. Direct server return

194. What does Amazon Route 53 use to enable low-latency and fault-tolerant architectures?
A. DNS Failover
B. Secure Sockets Layer

C. Virtual Private Network

D. Auto Scaling

195. Which service is NOT directly associated with Amazon Route 53?

A. DNS Management

B. Traffic Management

C. Availability Monitoring

D. Elastic Compute Cloud

196. What is the purpose of a bastion host in AWS?

A. To serve as a storage device

B. To provide a database service

C. To act as a proxy for accessing EC2 instances

D. To distribute web traffic evenly

197. Where is a bastion host typically located?

A. Inside a private network

B. On the outside of a firewall or in a DMZ

C. In an isolated AWS Region

D. Within an Internet Gateway

198. What is the advantage of using a NAT Gateway over a NAT instance?

A. Higher security features

B. Higher bandwidth and better availability

C. Ability to host web applications

D. Direct control over routing policies

199. What is the function of a NAT instance or gateway within a VPC?

A. To enable direct access to the Internet for public subnets

B. To allow instances in private subnets to access the Internet

C. To provide static IP addresses for instances

D. To encrypt data transferring between instances

200. What security practice is recommended for a bastion host?

A. Enabling auto-scaling

B. Hardening the bastion host

C. Installing a web server

D. Configuring it as a mail server

201. What is the primary function of AWS Cloud Map?

A. To monitor application health

B. To provide a firewall service

C. To manage AWS resources pricing

D. For service discovery and resource location tracking

202. How does AWS Cloud Map enhance application availability?

A. By providing a managed firewall service

B. By offering a relational database service

C. By performing deep packet inspection

D. By continuously monitoring the health of resources and updating their locations

203. What benefit does AWS Cloud Map provide to developers?

A. It automatically scales the database horizontally

B. It reduces the need to manually handle resource names and locations within the code

C. It replaces the need for a virtual private cloud

D. It introduces stateful rules for network traffic packets

204. Which AWS service is a stateful, managed network firewall and intrusion detection and prevention service?
A. AWS Cloud Map
B. AWS Network Firewall
C. AWS Relational Database Service (RDS)
D. AWS Direct Connect

205. What does the AWS Network Firewall use for stateful inspection?
A. AWS Firewall Manager
B. AWS Direct Connect
C. Suricata
D. AWS Relational Database Service (RDS)

206. What types of rules does AWS Network Firewall support?
A. Stateless and stateful rules
B. Deep packet inspection rules
C. NAT gateway rules
D. Relational database rules

207. How does AWS Network Firewall integrate with AWS Organizations?
A. Through AWS Cloud Map
B. With AWS Direct Connect
C. Using AWS Firewall Manager
D. Via Amazon Relational Database Service (RDS)

208. What are the types of databases supported by AWS-managed database services?
A. Relational and NoSQL databases
B. Firewall and Network databases
C. Static and Dynamic databases

D. Stateful and Stateless databases

209. What does the Amazon RDS Multi-AZ deployment feature provide?
A. Stateless packet inspection
B. A synchronously replicated standby instance for high availability
C. A registry for application service names
D. A firewall subnet for traffic filtering

210. When would you consider using a NoSQL database instead of a relational database with AWS?
A. When your application requires complex transactions and joins
B. When your application does not need joins or complex transactions
C. When you need to perform a stateful inspection of network traffic
D. When you need to manage firewall configurations across multiple accounts

211. What is the primary purpose of Amazon Simple Queue Service (SQS)?
A. To manage relational databases
B. To facilitate the decoupling and scaling of microservices, distributed systems, and serverless applications
C. To provide cloud storage solutions
D. To host web applications

212. What does FIFO stand for in the context of Amazon SQS?
A. First Input First Output
B. Final In Final Out
C. First In First Out
D. Fast Input Fast Output

213. Which feature of Amazon SQS ensures that messages are processed exactly once?
A. Redundant infrastructure
B. Server-Side Encryption (SSE)
C. FIFO queues
D. High availability

214. How does Amazon SQS provide high message durability?
A. By saving messages on a single server with a backup
B. By encrypting messages with AWS KMS
C. By saving messages on multiple servers
D. By using a first-come-first-serve algorithm

215. What is the maximum size of a message that Amazon SQS can directly handle?
A. 256 KB
B. 2 MB
C. 1 GB
D. 500 KB

216. What does Amazon SQS use to allow the transmission of sensitive data securely?
A. AWS Key Management Service (AWS KMS)
B. SSL/TLS encryption
C. Multi-factor authentication
D. Virtual Private Cloud (VPC)

217. Which of the following is NOT a benefit of using Amazon SQS?
A. On-premises deployment
B. Scalability

C. Reliability

D. Availability

218. What allows Amazon SQS to scale transparently to handle demand surges or spikes?

A. Manual provisioning

B. Predefined capacity limits

C. Individual processing of each delayed request

D. Scheduled scaling actions

219. Which AWS service can be used in conjunction with Amazon SQS to store the contents of messages larger than 256 KB?

A. Amazon RDS

B. Amazon S3

C. Amazon EC2

D. Amazon EBS

220. Which messaging service is recommended for new applications requiring practically unlimited scalability and straightforward APIs?

A. Amazon MQ

B. Amazon EC2

C. Amazon SQS and Amazon SNS

D. Amazon RDS

221. What is AWS DocumentDB compatible with?

A. MySQL

B. PostgreSQL

C. Oracle

D. MongoDB

222. Which of the following is NOT a feature of AWS DocumentDB?
A. Storage auto-scaling
B. Automatic failover to up to 15 replicas
C. Storage scales downwards automatically
D. Indexing of JSON data structures

223. What is a primary use case for AWS DocumentDB?
A. High-frequency stock trading
B. Social media profiles
C. Real-time multiplayer gaming
D. Time-series data analysis

224. Amazon ElastiCache is compatible with which caching engines?
A. Redis and Oracle Coherence
B. Redis and Memcached
C. Memcached and MySQL Cache
D. Redis and MongoDB

225. What is the main benefit of ElastiCache Auto-Discovery for Memcached?
A. It allows for automatic scaling of the cache size.
B. It enables automatic detection and recovery of cache node failures.
C. It lets applications discover and connect to nodes in a cache cluster.
D. It automatically updates Memcached to the latest version.

226. Which feature of AWS ElastiCache improves reliability for production deployments?
A. Auto-Discovery for cache engines
B. Automatic failover to a standby instance
C. In-memory data storage

VERSAtile Reads

D. Automatic detection and recovery of node failures

227. In ElastiCache for Redis, what is the cornerstone structure called?
A. Parameter group
B. Security group
C. Cluster
D. Node type

228. What does running an ElastiCache cluster in a VPC (Virtual Private Cloud) allow you to control?
A. The Redis engine version only
B. The geographic location of the data center
C. IP address range, subnets, and routing
D. The instance types of Amazon EC2 instances only

229. What is the purpose of a Multi-AZ deployment in AWS?
A. To reduce costs by sharing resources across regions
B. To provide data redundancy and failover capabilities
C. To increase storage capacity automatically
D. To enhance the performance of single-zone deployments

230. Which AWS service helps in monitoring the performance and health of an ElastiCache for the Redis cluster?
A. AWS CloudTrail
B. Amazon SNS
C. AWS CloudFormation
D. Amazon CloudWatch

231. Which AWS service is primarily used to migrate on-premises databases to AWS with minimal downtime?
A. Amazon Redshift

B. Amazon DataSync

C. Amazon Database Migration Service (DMS)

D. Amazon Simple Storage Service (S3)

232. What does AWS Schema Conversion Tool (AWS SCT) assist with during database migration?

A. Encrypting data at rest

B. Converting database schema to a different database engine

C. Transferring virtual machines to AWS

D. Incremental replication of server VMs

233. For which scenario is AWS Server Migration Service (SMS) best suited?

A. Transferring large volumes of data between on-premises and AWS

B. Migrating server VMs from on-premises server to AWS Cloud

C. Querying and analyzing large data sets

D. Migrating databases with no need for continuous replication

234. What is the main advantage of using AWS DataSync for data transfer?

A. It simplifies schema conversion during database migration.

B. It offers managed database services like Amazon RDS.

C. It accelerates transfers, making it significantly faster than open-source tools.

D. It automates the provisioning of data warehouse clusters.

235. Which AWS service is a fully managed, scalable cloud data warehouse?

A. AWS Glue

B. Amazon DynamoDB

C. Amazon Redshift

D. Amazon S3

236. Which AWS on-premises service is best described as a gigantic disk used to physically transfer large volumes of data to AWS?
A. AWS Storage Gateway
B. AWS Snowball
C. AWS Opsworks
D. AWS CodeDeploy

237. What feature differentiates Amazon Elastic File System (EFS) from Amazon Elastic Block Store (EBS)?
A. EFS is object-based storage.
B. EFS automatically resizes based on stored data.
C. EBS is a managed NoSQL database service.
D. EBS is used for deploying applications on-premises.

238. Which AWS service allows you to deploy your application code to both EC2 instances and on-premises web servers?
A. AWS Snowball Edge
B. AWS IoT Greengrass
C. AWS CodeDeploy
D. AWS Opsworks

239. Which AWS service is designed to orchestrate multi-server migrations and manage the status of servers comprising an application?
A. Amazon DataSync
B. AWS Server Migration Service (SMS)
C. AWS Database Migration Service (DMS)
D. Amazon S3

240. AWS on-premises services: what does the AWS Storage Gateway primarily provide?
A. It is a physical storage device similar to Snowball Edge.

B. It is a hybrid cloud service that caches files and replicates them to S3.

C. It facilitates schema conversion during database migration.

D. It deploys Lambda functions on-premises

241. What is the primary purpose of AWS PrivateLink?

A. To connect VPCs to the public internet

B. To enable public access to AWS services

C. To connect to AWS services using private IP addresses within your VPC

D. To replace the need for an AWS Transit Gateway

242. Which AWS service is recommended for connecting thousands of VPCs without requiring VPC peering?

A. AWS Direct Connect

B. AWS PrivateLink

C. AWS Transit Gateway

D. AWS VPN

243. What component is required on the service VPC for AWS PrivateLink to function?

A. Elastic Load Balancer

B. Network Load Balancer

C. Virtual Private Gateway

D. Internet Gateway

244. How many Transit Gateways can you connect at a time for hybrid connectivity via a single Direct Connect Connection?

A. One

B. Two

C. Three

D. Unlimited

VERSAtile Reads

245. Which of the following is an advantage of using AWS Transit Gateway over Transit VPC?

A. Requires managing VPN connections individually

B. Increases latency

C. Eliminates the need for EC2-based software appliances for traffic routing

D. Provides lower bandwidth for inter-VPC communication

246. Which AWS service is a managed version of Service Mesh?

A. AWS Direct Connect

B. AWS App Mesh

C. AWS VPN

D. AWS Elastic Load Balancing

247. In AWS App Mesh, what is a Virtual Node?

A. A DNS endpoint for connecting VPCs

B. A combination of a deployment and a service

C. A route within a Virtual Router

D. A private IP address used by AWS PrivateLink

248. What does AWS Transit Gateway use to control how traffic is routed among all connected networks?

A. Security Groups

B. NAT Gateways

C. Route Tables

D. Internet Gateways

249. What is the maximum burst speed for inter-VPC communication provided by AWS Transit Gateway?

A. 10 Gbps

B. 20 Gbps

C. 50 Gbps per Availability Zone

D. 100 Gbps

250. Which AWS service simplifies the management of connections between services over a network, particularly in microservices architectures?
A. AWS Lambda
B. AWS Fargate
C. AWS App Mesh
D. AWS Elastic Beanstalk

251. What is the primary responsibility of the cloud provider in the AWS Shared Responsibility Model?
A. Securing user data
B. Managing in-cloud software applications
C. Securing the underlying infrastructure of the cloud
D. Patching customer's content and applications

252. Which AWS service provides access-controlled compliance and security documents?
A. AWS Inspector
B. AWS Shield
C. AWS Artifact
D. AWS WAF

253. Which of the following is NOT a benefit of AWS Security?
A. Scaling the environment quickly
B. Automatic PCI DSS compliance for customers
C. Savings on money due to no upfront expenses
D. The ability to meet various compliance requirements

254. Which AWS compliance certification relates to healthcare information?
A. FedRAMP
B. HIPAA/HITECH
C. GDPR
D. ISO 27001

255. What does AWS manage in relation to 'managed services' like Amazon RDS or Amazon DynamoDB?
A. User content and applications
B. Physical security of data centers
C. Database patching and firewall configuration
D. Customer's network configurations

256. Which AWS compliance program is focused on online payment standards?
A. SOC 1
B. SOC 2
C. PCI DSS Level 1
D. NIST 800-171

257. What does ISO 27001 certify in terms of security management?
A. Payment card industry data security
B. Health information security
C. Security management best practices
D. Cloud service data encryption standards

258. How can users access AWS Artifact and view compliance reports?
A. By logging into the AWS Management Console and navigating to the "Security, Identity, & Compliance" section
B. By requesting physical copies from AWS support

C. Via AWS Command Line Interface only

D. Through a dedicated AWS Artifact mobile application

259. What is the significance of AWS having a wide range of compliance programs and certifications?

A. It ensures AWS services are suitable only for European regulations

B. It limits the use of AWS to government institutions

C. It helps customers satisfy compliance requirements globally

D. It allows AWS to operate independently of international standards

260. According to AWS's shared responsibility model, who is responsible for security within the cloud?

A. AWS exclusively

B. Third-party security services

C. The customer

D. Internet service providers

261. What is AWS Shield?

A. A data storage service

B. A managed DDoS protection service

C. A content delivery network

D. An email-sending service

262. What are the two tiers of AWS Shield?

A. Basic and Premium

B. Standard and Advanced

C. Free and Paid

D. Essential and Professional

263. What does AWS Shield Standard protect against?
A. Advanced persistent threats
B. Software vulnerabilities
C. Common Infrastructure attacks
D. Malware attacks

264. How does AWS Shield Advanced provide enhanced protection?
A. By encrypting data
B. Through flow-based monitoring of network traffic
C. By offering a virtual firewall
D. By providing secure email services

265. What is the cost of AWS Shield Advanced?
A. $1,000 per month
B. $2,000 per month
C. $3,000 per month
D. $4,000 per month

266. Who can access AWS Shield Advanced?
A. All AWS customers
B. AWS Free Tier customers
C. AWS Business Support and AWS Enterprise Support customers
D. AWS Shield Standard users

267. What type of service is AWS Shield Standard?
A. A subscription-based service
B. An add-on service with additional costs
C. A free service
D. A standalone paid service

268. What is the purpose of AWS Shield?

A. To optimize the performance of web applications

B. To provide automatic inline mitigations against DDoS attacks

C. To create web applications quickly

D. To monitor user activity on web applications

269. What is a DDoS attack?

A. An attack that steals user data

B. A malicious attempt to disrupt a system's availability by overwhelming it with traffic

C. A software bug that crashes applications

D. An unauthorized access attempt

270. AWS Shield Standard is designed to maintain what aspect of applications on AWS?

A. The security of application data

B. The high availability of applications

C. The low cost of application hosting

D. The scalability of applications

271. What is the primary use of AWS CloudWatch?

A. To manage cryptographic keys

B. To set up and govern a multi-account AWS environment

C. To monitor AWS resource performance

D. To continuously monitor for malicious activity

272. Which AWS service is used for detailed configuration tracking of AWS resources?

A. AWS Config

B. AWS Security Hub

C. AWS Control Tower

D. AWS Parameter Store

273. How many AWS services can you perform penetration testing on without prior approval?

A. Four

B. Six

C. Eight

D. Ten

274. What is the difference between AWS KMS and AWS CloudHSM?

A. KMS is used for threat detection, while CloudHSM is used for key management.

B. KMS is a multi-tenant service, while CloudHSM is single-tenant.

C. KMS is for setting up multi-account environments. CloudHSM isn't.

D. KMS complies with FIPS 140-2 level 3, while CloudHSM does not.

275. What does AWS Secrets Manager primarily help with?

A. Monitoring AWS resource configurations

B. Managing and rotating secrets for access to applications and services

C. Aggregating security data from AWS accounts

D. Storing strings and application configuration

276. What is a key benefit of using AWS Control Tower?

A. It provides threat detection across AWS accounts.

B. It offers a managed ETL service for data transformation.

C. It sets up and governs a secure, multi-account AWS environment.

D. It stores encrypted parameters for configuration and secrets.

277. Which AWS service offers continuous threat detection to protect accounts and data?

A. AWS Config
B. AWS CloudWatch
C. AWS GuardDuty
D. AWS KMS

278. What happens when IAM credentials are considered compromised?
A. AWS Secrets Manager rotates them.
B. AWS automatically deletes them.
C. They must be invalidated and replaced manually.
D. AWS Control Tower manages them.

279. What is the significance of the AWS Glue Data Catalog?
A. It stores encrypted parameters.
B. It is a managed ETL service.
C. It aggregates security findings.
D. It acts as a central schema repository.

280. What is the key difference between AWS Parameter Store and AWS Secrets Manager?
A. Parameter Store is for threat detection, while Secrets Manager is for key management.
B. Parameter Store is free with a limit on parameters, while Secrets Manager is paid without such limits.
C. Secrets Manager is used for multi-account setups, while Parameter Store is not.
D. Parameter Store is for continuous monitoring, while Secrets Manager is for configuration management.

281. What is the primary purpose of Amazon Athena?
A. To manage user identities in AWS
B. To detect and classify sensitive data

C. To run big data frameworks like Hadoop and Spark

D. To analyze data in S3 using standard SQL

282. Which of the following data formats is NOT supported by Amazon Athena?

A. ORC

B. Parquet

C. XML

D. JSON

283. What is Amazon Macie primarily used for?

A. Processing and analyzing massive volumes of data

B. Automatic detection, classification, and protection of sensitive data in AWS

C. Querying log files stored in S3

D. Managing ETL (Extract, Transform and Load) jobs

284. What AWS service is used with Amazon Athena to manage metadata?

A. Amazon Redshift

B. AWS Glue

C. Amazon RDS

D. AWS Lambda

285. Which of the following is NOT a feature of Amazon Athena?

A. It is a managed cluster platform.

B. It supports DDL using Hive.

C. It is serverless.

D. It is designed for 99.99999% durability.

VERSAtile Reads

286. What does PII stand for?
A. Public Internet Interface
B. Personally Identifiable Information
C. Private Identification Inference
D. Protected Instance Information

287. Which of the following is a use case for Amazon Athena?
A. Automating data classification
B. Running an ETL job
C. Analyzing AWS cost and usage reports
D. Monitoring and discovering security changes

288. What feature of Amazon Macie utilizes Natural Language Processing?
A. Data processing for analytics
B. Classifying different data types and content
C. Managing user identities
D. Querying structured data stores

289. Which AWS service is known for using machine learning to review data actions within an AWS account?
A. Amazon Athena
B. AWS Glue
C. Amazon EMR
D. Amazon Macie

290. What can Amazon EMR be used for?
A. To detect and classify sensitive data
B. To analyze data in S3 using SQL
C. To run big data frameworks like Hadoop and Spark for data processing and analysis
D. To automatically classify new data stored in Amazon S3

291. What is the primary responsibility of AWS customers under the shared responsibility model?
A. To secure the underlying AWS infrastructure
B. To manage the security of the operating system and applications
C. To ensure AWS complies with all certifications and attestations
D. To monitor and protect the AWS global infrastructure

292. Which AWS Trusted Advisor check helps to identify idle resources?
A. Performance Analyzer
B. Cost Optimization
C. Security Review
D. Fault Tolerance Analysis

293. For which type of AWS services does the customer not need to worry about configuration work?
A. IaaS services like Amazon EC2
B. AWS-managed services like Amazon RDS
C. Services requiring compliance with HIPAA
D. Services using AWS CloudTrail for logging

294. What is required to comply with the Payment Card Industry Data Security Standard (PCI DSS) Level 1?
A. Encrypting all data at rest and in transit
B. Regularly auditing AWS infrastructure
C. Entities dealing with online payments must be PCI DSS Level 1 compliant
D. Implementing Multi-Factor Authentication for all accounts

295. What action is encouraged or required by the AWS Acceptable Use Policy (AUP) for users who detect violations?
A. To immediately stop using AWS services

B. To report any violations or suspected security vulnerabilities

C. To handle the situation themselves without AWS intervention

D. To upgrade their service plan for better security

296. Which of the following is an example of a compliance certification or attestation that AWS undergoes?

A. GDPR

B. ISO 27001

C. AWS WAF

D. AWS IAM

297. Which AWS feature can intervene and block traffic in the event of a cross-site scripting attack using an SQL injection?

A. AWS Shield

B. AWS IAM

C. AWS WAF

D. AWS CloudTrail

298. What is the AWS Compliance Program primarily concerned with?

A. Enhancing the functionality of AWS services

B. Ensuring AWS customers adhere to the shared responsibility model

C. Providing certifications, complying with laws, regulations, and privacy, and aligning with frameworks

D. Monitoring user activity and reporting to legal authorities

299. What must AWS customers manage when using Infrastructure as a Service (IaaS) like Amazon EC2 and VPC?

A. The physical security of AWS data centers

B. The compliance and certifications of AWS services

C. All security configuration and management tasks

D. The AWS global infrastructure network

300. In the context of AWS, what does G-Cloud [UK] refer to?
A. A global network of AWS data centers
B. A cloud-based service for managing user access
C. A UK government framework for procuring cloud services
D. A security protocol for cloud-based applications

301. What is the primary purpose of Amazon Kinesis Video Streams?
A. To offer cloud storage solutions for video data.
B. To facilitate live video streaming from devices to the AWS Cloud.
C. To provide a service for video conferencing.
D. To encrypt video content for secure transfer.

302. Which data types can be streamed using Amazon Kinesis Video Streams?
A. Only video data.
B. Video and audio data.
C. Video, audio, and thermal imaging data.
D. Video, audio, thermal imaging, depth data, RADAR data, and other time-serialized data.

303. How can consumers process video streaming data using Amazon Kinesis Video Streams?
A. They must wait until the data is stored on S3.
B. They can only process data using third-party applications.
C. They can process the data in real-time or after it has been stored.
D. They are limited to processing data on Amazon EC2 instances.

304. What can you use Amazon Kinesis Data Analytics for?
A. To create and manage databases.

B. To process and analyze streaming data using SQL.

C. To monitor network traffic.

D. To conduct financial transactions.

305. Which AWS service helps in managing OpenSearch and Elasticsearch engines?

A. AWS Lambda.

B. AWS OpenSearch Service.

C. Amazon RDS.

D. Amazon EC2.

306. What kind of tasks does AWS OpenSearch Service handle for the user?

A. Video streaming and encryption.

B. Machine learning model training.

C. Software installation, setup, monitoring, and backups.

D. Real-time analytics and dashboard feeding.

307. Which of the following is a use case for AWS OpenSearch Service?

A. Email hosting.

B. Full-text search.

C. Blockchain management.

D. Virtual desktop environments

308. What is AWS Data Exchange primarily used for?

A. Deploying machine learning models.

B. Facilitating the discovery and subscription to third-party data.

C. Managing virtual cloud networks.

D. Hosting web applications.

309. How does AWS Data Exchange ensure data security and compliance?

A. By using a private cloud environment.

B. Through AWS Key Management Service (KMS) and IAM integration.

C. By restricting data usage to within AWS regions only.

D. By exclusively using dedicated physical servers.

310. What are the pricing models for AWS OpenSearch Service and AWS Data Exchange?

A. Fixed monthly subscriptions.

B. One-time payment for lifetime access.

C. Based on instance types, storage, data transfer, and additional features for AWS OpenSearch Service, Pay-As-You-Go for AWS Data Exchange.

D. Free for all AWS users.

311. What is the primary function of the Hadoop Distributed File System (HDFS) in AWS EMR architecture?

A. To manage cluster resources and schedule data processing tasks.

B. To serve as the main database for Amazon EMR.

C. To distribute data across cluster instances for fault tolerance.

D. To provide a platform for running SQL queries on large datasets.

312. How does Amazon EMR utilize EMRFS in relation to Amazon S3?

A. EMRFS is used as a primary database for Amazon EMR.

B. EMRFS allows Amazon EMR to directly access data stored in Amazon S3.

C. EMRFS synchronizes data between Amazon S3 and local file systems.

D. EMRFS is a tool for data visualization and analysis.

313. What is the default resource management system used by Amazon EMR?

A. Apache Spark

B. Amazon Data Pipeline

C. YARN (Yet Another Resource Negotiator)

D. Amazon QuickSight

314. Which of the following is NOT a component of AWS Data Pipeline?

A. Task Runner

B. Pipeline definition

C. Amazon S3

D. SPICE

315. What is the purpose of using AWS Data Pipeline?

A. To manage real-time data streaming.

B. To automate data transportation and transformation between different AWS services.

C. To create data visualizations and business insights.

D. To provide a file system interface for Amazon S3.

316. Which AWS service is primarily used to create visualizations and perform ad-hoc analysis?

A. AWS Data Pipeline

B. Amazon EMR

C. Amazon QuickSight

D. Amazon S3

317. What is the primary processing framework available for Amazon EMR?

A. Amazon Redshift

B. Apache Spark

C. Hadoop MapReduce

D. Both B and C

318. What does SPICE stand for in the context of Amazon QuickSight?
A. Simple Parallel Integrated Compute Engine
B. Super-fast, Parallel, In-memory Calculation Engine
C. Scalable Performance for Integrated Cloud Environments
D. Secure, Private, Isolated Compute Environment

319. In AWS EMR, what is the role of the local file system on each node?
A. To permanently store data like Amazon S3.
B. To store intermediate results of processing tasks.
C. To maintain the EMRFS metadata.
D. To store data that persists even after the cluster is terminated.

320. Which component of the AWS Data Pipeline is responsible for executing specified work activities?
A. Amazon EC2
B. Amazon S3
C. Pipeline
D. Task Runner

321. Which AWS service is used for creating speech and text-based conversational interfaces for applications?
A. Amazon Polly
B. Amazon Rekognition
C. Amazon Lex
D. Amazon Comprehend

322. What are the core technologies behind Amazon Lex?
A. Natural Language Processing (NLP) and Text-to-Speech (TTS)
B. Natural Language Understanding (NLU) and Automated Voice Recognition (ASR)
C. Image Recognition and Speech Synthesis

D. Machine Learning and Text Analysis

323. Which service is used to turn text into life-like speech?
A. AWS Lambda
B. Amazon Polly
C. Amazon Lex
D. Amazon Comprehend

324. What kind of insights can Amazon Comprehend provide from a document?
A. Entities, Key Phrases, PII, Language, Sentiment, Targeted Sentiment, Syntax
B. Speech Recognition, Text Translation, Sentiment Analysis, Language Identification
C. Image Recognition, Object Detection, Facial Analysis, Scene Detection
D. Text-to-Speech, Voice Selection, Language Translation

325. What is the primary function of Amazon Rekognition?
A. To extract insights from text using NLP
B. To convert text into speech
C. To provide visual search and image recognition capabilities
D. To create conversational chatbots

326. How does Amazon Lex handle voice inputs?
A. By converting voice to text and understanding user intent
B. By providing a text-to-speech service
C. By using image recognition to process spoken words
D. By translating voice inputs into multiple languages

327. In Amazon Polly, what can you select for your speech output?
A. Different programming languages
B. Various entities and key phrases

C. Different languages, male or female voices, and accents

D. Custom entities and classification models

328. Which AWS service offers built-in integration with AWS Lambda, Amazon CloudWatch, and Amazon DynamoDB?

A. Amazon Polly

B. Amazon Lex

C. Amazon Comprehend

D. Amazon Rekognition

329. What does Amazon Comprehend use to extract information about the content of documents?

A. Text-to-Speech algorithms

B. Natural Language Processing (NLP)

C. Automated Speech Recognition (ASR)

D. Visual search algorithms

330. What are the sentiments that Amazon Comprehend can determine from a document?

A. Positive, Neutral, Negative, Mixed

B. Happy, Sad, Angry, Surprised

C. Confident, Uncertain, Doubtful, Clear

D. Professional, Casual, Formal, Informal

331. What is the primary function of Amazon Comprehend?

A. To provision virtual servers

B. To manage relational databases

C. To analyze and extract insights from documents

D. To store large amounts of data

332. Which of the following is NOT a feature of Amazon Comprehend?
A. Detect Key Phrases
B. Topic Modeling
C. Real-time database management
D. Analyze Syntax

333. What are the processing methods available in Amazon Comprehend for documents?
A. Synchronous and Asynchronous
B. Batch and Stream processing
C. FIFO and LIFO queues
D. Encryption and Decryption

334. How does Amazon SageMaker assist data scientists and developers?
A. By optimizing search engine algorithms
B. By providing an environment to build, train, and deploy machine learning models
C. By offering web hosting services
D. By translating languages in real-time

335. What is the typical machine learning workflow in Amazon SageMaker?
A. Generate Example Data, Train a Model, Deploy the Model
B. Configure Databases, Deploy Servers, Manage Traffic
C. Upload Content, Manage CDN, Analyze Metrics
D. Write Code, Debug Programs, Compile Software

336. What service does Amazon Translate provide?
A. Text-to-speech conversion
B. Neural Machine Translation
C. Data encryption and security

D. Email automation

337. What is the pricing advantage of Amazon Translate compared to traditional human translation?
A. It's always free
B. It's approximately 50% cheaper
C. It costs a fraction (0.05%) of the average human translation
D. It has a fixed monthly subscription fee

338. Which AWS service is a cloud-based IDE that allows code editing and debugging?
A. AWS Lambda
B. Amazon EC2
C. Amazon RDS
D. AWS Cloud9

339. What built-in feature does AWS Cloud9 offer for serverless app developers?
A. Managed NoSQL database service
B. Functions to create, debug, and deploy AWS Lambda functions
C. Automated code reviews
D. Continuous integration and deployment pipelines

340. How does AWS Cloud9 support collaborative development?
A. By providing a shared physical server for code storage
B. By allowing developers to access the development environment from any internet-connected device
C. By enabling automatic code deployment to production servers
D. By offering a centralized version control system

341. What is the purpose of an Amazon Virtual Private Cloud (Amazon VPC)?
A. To provide a shared cloud environment with other AWS users
B. To provision a logically isolated section of the AWS cloud for launching resources
C. To generate memes using AWS Lambda functions
D. To create a public-facing website without any customizable network options

342. What are some of the multiple connectivity options available in an Amazon VPC?
A. Connecting to a local database server only
B. Connecting directly to the internet using public subnets
C. Using a single internet gateway for all VPCs
D. Allowing public access to all subnets by default

343. Which feature enables EC2 instances in the EC2-Classic platform to communicate with instances in a VPC using private IP addresses?
A. Internet Gateway
B. NAT Gateway
C. VPC Peering Connection
D. VPC Endpoints

344. What is the purpose of an Internet Gateway in Amazon VPC?
A. To manage VPN connections exclusively
B. To connect VPC resources to an on-premises data center
C. To act as the VPC side of a connection to the public internet
D. To encrypt traffic between VPCs

345. What is AWS Lambda primarily used for?
A. Managing servers and clusters

B. Running code without provisioning or managing servers

C. Creating VPN connections

D. Logging network traffic through network interfaces

346. How can AWS Direct Connect benefit an organization?

A. By providing a shared internet connection with other AWS users

B. By establishing a less secure but faster connection to AWS

C. By offering a dedicated network connection from premises to AWS

D. By only allowing access to AWS Lambda

347. What is an Egress-only Internet Gateway used for in Amazon VPC?

A. To provide a dedicated connection to AWS services

B. To allow IPv6 traffic from the VPC to access the internet

C. To connect exclusively to on-premises networks

D. To offer stateless traffic management

348. Which of the following is NOT a component of Amazon VPC?

A. Subnet

B. Customer Gateway

C. Elastic Load Balancing

D. VPC Endpoints

349. What functionality does a NAT Gateway provide in a VPC?

A. To allow instances in a public subnet to access the internet

B. To enable direct internet access to all VPC resources

C. To manage inbound traffic from the internet

D. To allow resources in a private subnet to access the internet

350. In what scenario might you combine a VPN with AWS Direct Connect?

A. When a VPN connection is too reliable

B. When you do not require a dedicated line to AWS

C. When you need a more reliable connection to AWS with encryption

D. If you prefer to use internet-based connections

351. What is the purpose of AWS Batch?

A. To deploy web applications

B. To automate code deployments

C. To process large workloads in batches

D. To manage source control systems

352. Which AWS service provides a fully managed source control solution?

A. AWS CodeBuild

B. AWS CodeDeploy

C. AWS CodePipeline

D. Amazon CodeCommit

353. What can you define in an AWS Batch Job Definition?

A. The operating system for the computing environment

B. The source control repository URL

C. The Docker container images for running jobs

D. The AWS CodePipeline stages

354. Which AWS service is used for automated code deployments?

A. AWS CodeBuild

B. AWS CodeDeploy

C. AWS CodeCommit

D. Amazon S3

355. What does AWS CodeBuild primarily do?

A. Manages to build servers

B. Stores and versions code

C. Deploys applications to production

D. Builds source code and runs unit tests

356. How does AWS CodeDeploy help maintain application uptime?

A. By providing a source control repository

B. By managing user access to applications

C. By performing in-place updates with rolling deployments

D. By offering prepackaged build environments

357. Which of the following is NOT a computing platform supported by AWS CodeDeploy?

A. Amazon EC2

B. Amazon S3

C. AWS Lambda

D. Amazon ECS

358. What is the key benefit of AWS CodePipeline?

A. It provides secure source control for Git repositories

B. It automates the software release process with continuous delivery

C. It processes large-scale batch computing workloads

D. It manages and scales build servers

359. When using AWS Batch, what does the Job Queue do?

A. Stores Docker container images

B. Manages the source code repository

C. Routes submitted jobs to computing environments

D. Provides a managed source control environment

360. What can AWS CodeCommit be used to store?

A. EC2 instances

B. Build artifacts

C. Code, binaries, and version-controlled data

D. Batch computing software

361. What is the primary function of AWS Cloud9?
A. To provide machine learning services
B. To host static websites
C. To run a web-based integrated development environment
D. To store large data sets for big data analysis

362. What type of environment does AWS Cloud9 create when it launches an Amazon EC2 instance for you?
A. Lambda environment
B. EC2 environment
C. SSH environment
D. CodeCommit environment

363. Which AWS service provides AI-powered enterprise search capabilities?
A. Amazon Textract
B. Amazon Transcribe
C. Amazon Rekognition
D. Amazon Kendra

364. What can Amazon Textract be used for?
A. Transcribing speech to text
B. Extracting text and data from documents
C. Searching through enterprise content
D. Recognizing objects in images

365. How does Amazon Transcribe provide real-time speech recognition?
A. By converting text to speech
B. By recognizing objects in images

C. By analyzing audio streams and returning transcripts in real-time
D. By extracting data from forms and tables

366. What feature of Amazon Rekognition can be used to identify and analyze faces?
A. Object detection
B. Facial analysis
C. Scene detection
D. Language recognition

367. What type of AWS Cloud9 environment is created when linking to an existing cloud computing instance or your server?
A. EC2 environment
B. Lambda environment
C. SSH environment
D. Glacier environment

368. What is the proposed solution for Cleveland Medical Center's challenge of identifying patients by face?
A. Deploying Amazon Textract
B. Using Amazon Transcribe
C. Implementing Amazon Kendra
D. Utilizing Amazon Rekognition facial analysis

369. What is the advantage of a "Cloud First" strategy, as advised for Cleveland Medical Center?
A. It relies on on-premises IT resources.
B. It requires a significant upfront investment.
C. It offers scalability and reduces wasted resources.
D. It is only suitable for small-scale operations.

370. What is the advantage of saving the environment in the cloud?
A. It enhances machine learning capabilities.
B. It restricts access to a single machine or server setup.
C. It allows for easy swapping between computers and rapid onboarding of developers.
D. It increases the need for local storage of project files

371. What type of architecture does AWS Lambda represent?
A. Monolithic Architecture
B. Microservices Architecture
C. Serverless Architecture
D. Traditional Architecture

372. In AWS Lambda, what service is used to trigger Lambda functions through API calls?
A. EC2 Instances
B. Elastic Load Balancer
C. API Gateway
D. DynamoDB

373. Which AWS database service is typically used in a truly serverless architecture with AWS Lambda?
A. MySQL
B. Oracle RDS
C. Microsoft SQL Server
D. DynamoDB

374. How many requests can AWS Lambda handle for free before incurring charges?
A. 500,000 requests

B. 1 million requests

C. 2 million requests

D. 10 million requests

375. What is the pricing model for AWS Lambda based on execution duration?

A. $0.00001667 per GB-second used

B. $0.00000200 per GB-second used

C. $0.00000100 per GB-second used

D. $0.00001000 per GB-second used

376. Which of the following is NOT a supported programming language for AWS Lambda?

A. Ruby

B. Node.js

C. Python

D. Go

377. What feature of AWS Lambda allows for rolling back to previous versions of your code?

A. Elastic Load Balancing

B. Version Control

C. API Gateway

D. DynamoDB Integration

378. Under the shared responsibility model, what is Amazon responsible for in Lambda?

A. Programming language version

B. Application code

C. Hardware and OS maintenance

D. API Gateway configuration

379. What is the scaling behavior of AWS Lambda?
A. Scales up automatically
B. Scales down automatically
C. Scales out automatically
D. Does not scale

380. What does it mean that you are only charged for the computing time you consume?
A. You are billed monthly for a fixed number of compute hours.
B. You are charged only when your Lambda function is actively running code.
C. You pay a flat rate for unlimited computing time.
D. You purchase compute time in advance and are refunded for unused minutes.

381. What is the maximum number of containers you can define in an AWS Fargate task definition?
A. 5
B. 10
C. 15
D. 20

382. What is the purpose of Amazon ECS clusters in relation to AWS Fargate?
A. To provide a physical server for task deployment
B. To group tasks or services for application isolation
C. To manage user access and permissions
D. To store container images

VERSAtile Reads

383. When using AWS Fargate, what do you NOT need to worry about?
A. Selecting server types
B. Scaling clusters
C. Optimizing cluster packing
D. All of the above

384. What does Amazon Lightsail include for project deployment?
A. Only virtual machines
B. Containers and databases only
C. A complete suite including virtual machines, storage, and networking capacity
D. Just DNS management tools

385. What are AWS Outposts primarily used for?
A. To run fully managed databases
B. To provide a hybrid deployment model with on-premises cloud services
C. To host static websites
D. To offer a serverless environment

386. What kind of projects is Amazon Lightsail best suited for?
A. Large enterprise applications
B. Projects requiring many virtual private servers
C. Small projects with quick deployments
D. High-computing AI research projects

387. Which AWS service is considered serverless and is used to manage containers?
A. Amazon EC2
B. AWS Lambda
C. AWS Fargate

D. Amazon S3

388. How does AWS Outposts connect to your on-premises network?
A. Through a direct satellite link
B. Using a dedicated fiber optic cable
C. By establishing a connection to an AWS Region
D. Through a public internet connection only

389. What component extends an Amazon VPC from an AWS Region to an Outpost?
A. Internet Gateways
B. Local Gateways
C. Outpost Subnets
D. VPC Peering

390. What is the purpose of the Amazon Route 53 DNS Service for EC2 instances in Outposts subnets?
A. To provide a static IP address
B. To resolve domain names to IP addresses
C. To manage data transfer costs
D. To offer dedicated host capabilities

391. What is the primary purpose of AWS CodePipeline?
A. To automate application deployment
B. To provide data storage solutions
C. To manage AWS user permissions
D. To collect data about requests served by your application

392. Which AWS service is primarily used for debugging and analyzing production applications?
A. AWS CodeCommit

B. AWS CodeBuild

C. AWS CodeStar

D. AWS X-Ray

393. What is a 'stage' in the context of AWS CodePipeline?

A. A specific AWS region where the pipeline is deployed

B. A logical unit within a pipeline consisting of one or more actions

C. The final production environment

D. A single task within a pipeline

394. Which of the following AWS services allows developers to collaboratively work on development projects?

A. AWS CodeDeploy

B. AWS CodeStar

C. AWS CodeBuild

D. Amazon CodeArtifact

395. What is an 'action' in AWS CodePipeline?

A. A trigger that starts the pipeline execution

B. A permission policy for accessing pipeline resources

C. An operation performed on application code at a certain stage in the pipeline

D. A notification is sent when a pipeline stage completes

396. How can a pipeline execution be stopped in AWS CodePipeline?

A. By removing all stages from the pipeline

B. By deleting the AWS CodePipeline service from the account

C. By manually halting the execution or through automated rules

D. By archiving the pipeline

VERSAtile Reads

397. What is the role of AWS CodeArtifact?
A. To manage continuous integration and deployment
B. To provide a package management service
C. To offer compute capacity for running applications
D. To collect and analyze user behavior data

398. What is a 'pipeline' in the context of AWS CodePipeline?
A. A virtual network for secure communication between AWS services
B. A collection of AWS resources provisioned for an application
C. A procedural concept outlining how software updates are released
D. A storage location for deployment artifacts

399. Which AWS service provides a centralized project dashboard for managing development projects?
A. Amazon S3
B. AWS CodePipeline
C. AWS CodeStar
D. Amazon EC2

400. In AWS CodePipeline, what is a 'source revision'?
A. A new feature added to the pipeline
B. A backup of the pipeline's configuration
C. A version of the source change that triggers a pipeline execution
D. The original code before any pipeline modifications

401. What is the primary purpose of AWS Direct Connect?
A. To manage AWS services using the AWS Management Console
B. To secure browsing activities on the internet
C. To create a dedicated network connection from a remote network to

AWS
D. To provide static IP addresses for applications

402. What are the primary benefits of using AWS Direct Connect?
A. Cost reduction and increased reliability
B. Static IP address provisioning
C. Acceleration of global traffic
D. Securing internet browsing activities

403. Which of the following AWS services can be accessed via AWS Direct Connect using a public virtual interface (VIF)?
A. EC2 and Amazon VPC
B. S3 and EC2 using public IP addresses
C. Application Load Balancer and Network Load Balancer
D. VPN connections

404. What does AWS Direct Connect use to establish a connection from a data center to AWS?
A. A VPN over the internet
B. A fiber optic cable connection
C. Static IP addresses
D. AWS Management Console

405. How is data transfer into an AWS account charged when using AWS Direct Connect with private VIFs?
A. It is charged per GB at the standard internet data transfer rate.
B. It is free of charge.
C. It is charged at a higher rate compared to public VIFs.
D. It is included in the port hour charges

406. Which component of AWS Global Accelerator provides a set of Static IP addresses from the AWS edge network?
A. Network zone
B. Accelerator
C. Endpoint group
D. Listener

407. What can you control in AWS Global Accelerator to adjust the percentage of traffic directed to an endpoint group?
A. Accelerator settings
B. Listener configurations
C. The traffic dial
D. Endpoint weights

408. In AWS Global Accelerator, what is the purpose of an endpoint?
A. To provide static IP addressing
B. To act as a fixed entry point for client applications
C. To serve as the destination for routed traffic
D. To monitor the health of the application

409. What type of connection does AWS Direct Connect allow for accessing Amazon VPC without involving the internet?
A. Public VIF based
B. Static IP based
C. VPN connection
D. Private VIF based

410. What is the primary difference between AWS Direct Connect and a VPN Connection?
A. VPN Connection uses a dedicated line, while Direct Connect uses the internet.
B. Direct Connect is for public IP addresses, while VPN is for private IP

addresses.

C. Direct Connect uses a dedicated connection, while VPN uses the internet.

D. VPN Connection is more reliable than Direct Connect.

411. What was the change made to IT assets in October 2018?

A. IT assets became non-programmable

B. IT assets were converted to physical servers

C. IT assets were changed from programmable to provisioned resources

D. IT assets were made available only in certain regions

412. What does cloud scalability refer to?

A. The ability of a system to reduce costs

B. The ability of a system to respond and adjust to evolving requests

C. The time it takes to deploy an application globally

D. The security measures taken by cloud services

413. Which AWS service is used to manage infrastructure as code?

A. AWS Lambda

B. AWS Elastic Beanstalk

C. AWS CloudFormation

D. Amazon EC2

414. What is a golden image in AWS?

A. A public image available for all AWS users

B. A premium image with pre-installed software for high costs

C. A snapshot of a particular state of a resource

D. An algorithm used by AWS Lambda

415. How can AWS CloudWatch Alarms be used?

A. To monitor the usage of EC2 instances

B. To send an Amazon SNS message when a metric crosses a threshold

C. To manage user permissions and policies

D. To register domain names

416. What is the purpose of Amazon Route 53?

A. To manage user access and permissions

B. To register and manage domain names

C. To automate the scaling of EC2 instances

D. To store large amounts of data

417. What type of application does not need knowledge of previous interactions?

A. Stateful application

B. Stateless application

C. Scalable application

D. Secure application

418. Which AWS service provides a serverless architecture?

A. AWS EC2

B. AWS RDS

C. AWS Lambda

D. AWS S3

419. What are the two ways to scale systems in AWS?

A. Scale Up and Scale Down

B. Scale In and Scale Out

C. Scale Up and Scale Out

D. Scale Forward and Scale Back

420. What is the benefit of using AWS-managed services?
A. They offer physical servers on rent
B. They provide managed services for a fixed contract term
C. They help organizations move faster and lower IT costs
D. They solely focus on providing high-network architecture

421. What is the primary purpose of the AWS Application Discovery Service?
A. To provide data backup solutions
B. To facilitate on-premises data center migration planning to AWS
C. To offer managed blockchain services
D. To deploy new applications on AWS

422. Which AWS service is known for its scalability and resilience, automatically adjusting to varying storage needs without downtime?
A. Amazon EC2
B. Amazon S3
C. Amazon RDS
D. Amazon DynamoDB

423. What does the AWS Application Discovery Service's Agentless Discovery Connector do?
A. Manages private 5G networks
B. Provides a visual interface for machine learning models
C. Identifies VMs and hosts associated with VMware vCenter
D. Offers a centralized platform for game management

424. What is Amazon Redshift Serverless designed to do?
A. Automatically scale compute clusters based on workload predictions
B. Scan palms for secure access control
C. Manage private 5G networks
D. Offer quantum computing applications

425. Which AWS service uses a unique combination of palm and vein imagery for identity verification?
A. Amazon Aurora Limitless Database
B. Amazon One Enterprise
C. AWS Amplify Studio
D. Amazon GameSparks LiveOps

426. What type of tool is Amazon Q within AWS QuickSight?
A. A multi-faceted tool for storage solutions
B. A conversational AI assistant
C. A generative BI capabilities feature
D. A platform for managing mobile and web applications

427. What is the AWS Transit Gateway Connect's main function?
A. To simplify the connection of on-premises networks to Amazon VPCs and Transit Gateways
B. To offer a fully managed NAS solution
C. To enable searching within documents stored in S3
D. To provide a service for threat detection and incident response

428. What does Amazon ElastiCache Serverless remove the need for?
A. Capacity planning and manual patching
B. Enterprise-level security
C. Blockchain services
D. Game management

429. How does Amazon Q serve as a digital assistant in its Generative AI Assistant form?
A. By offering unmatched performance and low latency for data
B. By helping employees with tasks like answering questions and

generating content

C. By providing a centralized platform for analytics and player engagement in games

D. By enabling the building and scaling of mobile and web applications

430. What is the main advantage of using Amazon EBS Snapshots on Amazon S3 Glacier Deep Archive?

A. It provides a managed blockchain service

B. It offers a high-performance computing environment

C. It enables the creation of private 5G networks

D. It offers long-term storage at a low cost

431. What does AWS's "Pay as you go" pricing policy entail?

A. Pay a fixed monthly fee regardless of usage

B. Pay a one-time upfront cost for lifelong service

C. Pay only for the computing resources you use

D. Pay for a minimum set amount of resources each month

432. Which pricing model offers up to 60% savings over On-demand capacity in AWS?

A. Pay less when you reserve

B. Pay as you go

C. Custom pricing

D. Pay even less as AWS grows

433. Which AWS API can be used to query specific pricing information for services like Amazon EC2 instances in a particular region?

A. AWS Price List Bulk API

B. AWS Price List Query API

C. AWS Simple Notification Service API

D. AWS Management Console

434. Which AWS service provides a free, hands-on experience with the AWS platform, products, and services for new customers?
A. AWS Free Tier
B. AWS Elastic Beanstalk
C. AWS Identity and Access Management (IAM)
D. AWS CloudFormation

435. Which AWS service is free to use, but the resources that it provisions are not?
A. AWS Elastic Beanstalk
B. Amazon VPC
C. Auto Scaling
D. AWS OpsWorks

436. What are the three fundamental characteristics you will be charged for when using the AWS Cloud platform?
A. Compute, Storage, and Data Transfer Out
B. User Access, Security, and API Calls
C. Support Plans, Software Packages, and Region
D. Load Balancing, Monitoring, and Elastic IPs

437. Which type of Amazon EC2 purchase option provides significant discounts with a low one-off or no upfront payment?
A. On-Demand Instances
B. Reserved Instances
C. Spot Instances
D. Dedicated Hosts

438. Which AWS service allows you to visualize and manage your AWS costs and usage over time?

A. AWS Budgets
B. AWS Cost Explorer
C. AWS Price List API
D. AWS Trusted Advisor

439. What is the benefit of using Consolidated Billing in AWS?
A. It provides free storage for consolidated account data.
B. It offers automatic scaling for accounts based on usage.
C. It combines billing for all accounts to obtain tiering benefits.
D. It allows for unlimited free data transfers within the same region.

440. Which factor does not affect the cost of Amazon S3?
A. Storage Class
B. The number of objects stored
C. Geographic region of your bucket
D. Data Transfer Out

441. What is the maximum number of tags that most AWS resources can have?
A. 10
B. 20
C. 50
D. 100

442. When can you add tags to an AWS resource?
A. Only at the creation of the resource
B. Within 24 hours of creating the resource
C. Anytime after the resource is created
D. Both A and C are correct.

443. Which AWS feature allows you to add tags to multiple resources at once?
A. AWS Management Console
B. AWS CLI
C. Tag Editor
D. AWS SDK

444. Can you edit tag keys and values after assigning them to a resource?
A. Yes, but only within 30 days
B. No, tags are immutable once assigned
C. Yes, at any time
D. Yes, but only the values, not the keys

445. What happens to the tags of a resource if the resource is deleted?
A. The tags are archived
B. The tags are saved for future use
C. The tags are automatically transferred to a new resource
D. Any tags for the resource are deleted

446. How do tags function in AWS accounts?
A. As user accounts
B. As virtual firewalls
C. As resource properties
D. As billing gateways

447. What is one of the benefits of tagging AWS resources?
A. It decreases security
B. It simplifies resource and access management
C. It increases the cost of resources
D. It limits automation

448. What can you do by listing resources with specific tags?
A. Increase their storage size
B. Change their region
C. Execute management tasks at scale
D. Convert them into a different resource type

449. What is one scenario where resource tagging is particularly useful for automation?
A. To automate the creation of new resources
B. To automate the shutdown or removal of resources at the end of the working day
C. To automate the increase of resource pricing
D. To automate the geographical relocation of resources

450. What is the benefit of creating and implementing an AWS tagging standard across an organization?
A. It increases the complexity of the AWS environment
B. It ensures consistent management and governance of AWS environments
C. It restricts the types of resources that can be used
D. AWS requires it for all organizations

451. What is the primary purpose of a paying master account in AWS Organizations?
A. To deploy resources
B. To provide technical support
C. To serve as the central billing account
D. To manage user permissions

452. What is a significant advantage of using consolidated billing in AWS Organizations?
A. Increased complexity of tracking costs
B. Separate bills for each AWS account
C. Sharing volume pricing discounts across accounts
D. Additional fees for consolidated billing

453. What is the recommended use for the paying account in AWS Organizations?
A. It should be used for deploying resources.
B. It should be used for technical support services.
C. It should be used only for billing purposes.
D. It should be used for managing IAM roles and policies.

454. What is the soft limit of accounts you can have per AWS Organization?
A. 5 accounts
B. 10 accounts
C. 20 accounts
D. 50 accounts

455. How are volume discounts calculated with consolidated billing for AWS services like Amazon EC2 and S3?
A. Based on the usage of each account
B. By combining the usage from all accounts
C. By the number of active users in each account
D. Through a flat rate regardless of usage

456. What is the effect of consolidated billing on Reserved Instances in AWS Organizations?
A. Reserved Instances benefits are not shared across accounts.
B. Only the account that purchases Reserved Instances benefits from them.

Copyright © 2024 VERSAtile Reads. All rights reserved.
This material is protected by copyright, any infringement will be dealt with legal and punitive action. 114

C. Reserved Instances are reserved for the master account only.

D. Unused Reserved Instances benefits are applied across the organization.

457. What is the role of the AWS Billing Conductor?

A. To provide technical assistance for billing issues

B. To offer a customizable billing service to align with business logic

C. To deploy resources across multiple accounts

D. To limit the usage of AWS services

458. What do billing groups in AWS Billing Conductor provide?

A. A method to limit user permissions

B. Contextual understanding of consumption and costs by financial owners

C. A way to reduce the number of AWS accounts

D. A tool for technical support management

459. How can AWS Billing Conductor help with rate management?

A. By setting a fixed rate for all services

B. By preventing any changes to pricing

C. By allowing the creation of pricing rules to set end-user rates

D. By automatically reducing rates every month

460. How does AWS Billing Conductor handle commitment-based discounts like Savings Plans?

A. Commitment-based discounts are shared across all AWS accounts.

B. Only accounts in the billing group benefit if an account purchases them within the group.

C. Commitment-based discounts are exclusive to the master account.

D. Savings Plans cannot be shared and are only applied to the account that purchased them.

461. What is the primary purpose of the AWS Knowledge Center?
A. To sell AWS services
B. To provide a centralized resource for information on AWS
C. To host virtual AWS conferences
D. To offer discounts on AWS services

462. Which of the following is a key feature of the AWS Knowledge Center?
A. Extensive Documentation
B. Live customer support
C. Free AWS credits
D. Physical AWS training centers

463. What type of content can community members contribute?
A. Financial reports
B. User-generated insights, advice, and solutions
C. Promotional advertisements
D. Personal blog posts

464. How does the AWS Knowledge Center assist visual learners?
A. By providing video materials
B. By offering braille documentation
C. By sending information booklets
D. By organizing in-person seminars

465. What type of navigation does the AWS Knowledge Center offer to help users find specific information?
A. Alphabetical navigation
B. Topic-based navigation
C. Random navigation
D. Service-level navigation

466. What does AWS Professional Services specialize in?
A. Cloud-based game development
B. Social media management
C. Migration of applications to the cloud
D. Cryptocurrency trading

467. What is the vision of AWS Professional Services?
A. To be the most affordable cloud service provider
B. To be the most customer-focused professional services team in the IT industry
C. To have the largest data centers in the world
D. To offer the fastest internet speeds

468. What methodology does AWS Professional Services use?
A. Third-party methodologies
B. Competitor-based methodologies
C. Proprietary methodology based on Amazon's internal best practices
D. No specific methodology

469. What is the purpose of Resource Groups in AWS?
A. To provide financial assistance to AWS users
B. To organize resources by common tags for easy management
C. To group user accounts for billing purposes
D. To limit resource usage per region

470. What can Resource Groups display?
A. Only security group configurations
B. Metrics, alarms, and configuration details
C. Only CPU utilization metrics
D. Only user account information

471. Which AWS Support Plan includes a Technical Account Manager (TAM)?
A. Developer
B. Business
C. Enterprise On-Ramp
D. Enterprise

472. What is the response time for a Production System Down case under the Business Support Plan?
A. 12 hours
B. 4 hours
C. 1 hour
D. 15 minutes

473. Which feature is exclusive to the Enterprise Support Plan but NOT included in the Enterprise On-Ramp Plan?
A. Infrastructure event management
B. AWS Trusted Advisor
C. On-Site Support
D. AWS Concierge

474. What is the monthly cost for the Developer Support Plan?
A. Free
B. $29
C. $100
D. $5,500

475. Which AWS Support Plan is ideal for individuals and small businesses just starting with AWS?
A. Basic
B. Developer

C. Business

D. Enterprise

476. Under which AWS Support Plan do you get guidance on using AWS products, features, and services for non-production workloads?
A. Basic
B. Developer
C. Business
D. Enterprise On-Ramp

477. Which AWS Support Plan offers a response time of less than 15 minutes for a Business-Critical System Down case?
A. Developer
B. Business
C. Enterprise On-Ramp
D. Enterprise

478. What does the AWS Trusted Advisor provide to Business and Enterprise Support Plan customers?
A. Infrastructure event management
B. Recommendations for best practices and optimization
C. Dedicated customer service personnel
D. On-Site Support

479. Which AWS Support Plan is recommended for customers who rely on their business solutions to be available, scalable, and secured?
A. Basic
B. Developer
C. Business
D. Enterprise On-Ramp

480. Which AWS Support Plan offers proactive alerts and a dedicated account manager?
A. Developer
B. Business
C. Enterprise On-Ramp
D. Enterprise

481. What is the AWS Partner Network (APN)?
A. A network of AWS users
B. A global community of partners leveraging AWS offerings
C. A single AWS service
D. Amazon's internal development team

482. Which of the following are the two types of partners in APN?
A. APN Technology Partners and APN User Partners
B. APN Consulting Partners and APN Technology Partners
C. APN Service Partners and APN Channel Partners
D. APN Registered Partners and APN Advanced Partners

483. How can AWS partners advance to higher performance tiers?
A. By completing AWS certifications only
B. Through customer engagement, training, and monetary investments
C. By increasing their annual revenue
D. Solely by marketing AWS services

484. What are the performance tiers offered by AWS for APN Consulting Partners?
A. Starter, Intermediate, Professional, and Expert
B. Basic, Registered, Standard, and Advanced

C. Registered, Standard, Advanced, and Premier

D. Associate, Professional, Master, and Specialist

485. What is included in the AWS Test Drive program?

A. Free AWS credits for startups

B. Preconfigured server-based tools and workloads for testing

C. A guided tour of AWS data centers

D. Free AWS certification exams

486. What is the AWS CLI?

A. A tool for automated cloud storage

B. A web-based AWS management console

C. A centralized tool for managing AWS services from the command line

D. An AWS certification for developers

487. What are the benefits of using an SDK?

A. It only provides debugging tools

B. It increases development efficiency with pre-built components and libraries

C. It only offers tutorials and documentation

D. It reduces the number of programming languages needed

488. What is the primary purpose of an API?

A. To provide a set of operating system functionalities

B. To manage cloud storage and databases

C. To facilitate communication between applications

D. To offer pre-built modules and components for development

489. In which of the following scenarios would you use an SDK?

A. When you want to communicate between two different applications

B. When you need to install an operating system
C. When you are developing an application and need to use pre-built tools and libraries
D. When you are creating an API

490. Which of the following is NOT a typical component of a game development SDK?
A. 3D graphics libraries
B. Physical server hardware
C. Artificial intelligence libraries
D. Debugging tools

491. What is the primary function of the AWS SDK?
A. To provide a digital catalog of prebuilt solutions
B. To automate and orchestrate the configuration of resources across the AWS platform
C. To enable integration of AWS services into applications
D. To manage application configuration data centrally

492. Which AWS service provides continuous monitoring and recording of AWS resource configurations?
A. AWS Systems Manager
B. AWS Config
C. AWS CloudFormation
D. AWS OpsWorks

493. What are the three products in the AWS OpsWorks lineup?
A. AWS OpsWorks for Chef Automate, AWS Systems Manager, AWS OpsWorks Stacks
B. AWS OpsWorks for Puppet Enterprise, AWS Config, AWS OpsWorks Stacks
C. AWS OpsWorks for Chef Automate, AWS OpsWorks for Puppet

Enterprise, AWS Service Catalog
D. AWS OpsWorks for Chef Automate, AWS OpsWorks for Puppet
Enterprise, AWS OpsWorks Stacks

494. What is the benefit of using AWS Marketplace?
A. It offers a set of tools for deploying software across instances.
B. It automates server configurations with code.
C. It provides a curated digital catalog to find, buy, deploy, and manage
third-party software.
D. It enables centralized management of application configuration data.

495. Which pricing options are available on AWS Marketplace?
A. Free trial, bi-annual, and BYOL model
B. Hourly, monthly, annual, multi-year, and BYOL model
C. Weekly, quarterly, and BYOL model
D. Daily, bi-monthly, and BYOL model

496. Who can use AWS Marketplace as a consumer?
A. Only AWS employees
B. Any individual with an AWS account
C. Only AWS-certified developers
D. Only Independent Software Vendors (ISVs)

497. What is the role of AWS CloudFormation in AWS Configuration
Management?
A. It manages infrastructure as code.
B. It provides continuous monitoring and recording.
C. It offers tools for software deployment.
D. It enables centralized management of application configurations.

498. Which AWS service helps standardize and govern the provisioning of cloud resources?
A. AWS Config
B. AWS Systems Manager
C. AWS Service Catalog
D. AWS AppConfig

499. What must be verified about an SDK to ensure it does not pose security risks?
A. It comes from reputable sources and is free of dangerous code.
B. It only supports one programming language.
C. It is the most expensive option available.
D. It is only compatible with a single deployment infrastructure.

500. What should be considered regarding the SDK's licensing agreement when choosing an SDK?
A. It must allow for the unlimited creation of user accounts.
B. It should cover all required usage and comply with the law.
C. It should guarantee the SDK's compatibility with all programming languages.
D. It must include free trials for all software products.

Answers

1. Answer: C

Explanation: Cloud computing removes the need for significant capital expenses associated with purchasing and managing hardware and software and setting up and operating on-site data centers. This includes the costs of server racks, 24/7 electricity for power and cooling, and IT experts to manage the infrastructure.

2. Answer: C

Explanation: Cloud services can dynamically scale to meet the needs of its users. In the cloud, the resources can be increased or decreased as per demand, which provides a business with the flexibility to scale globally without worrying about the physical constraints of their local infrastructure.

3. Answer: C

Explanation: Cloud computing provides a substantial increase in agility for organizations since new IT resources are only a click away, which means a vast amount of computing resources can be provisioned in minutes, typically with just a few mouse clicks, giving businesses a lot of flexibility and taking the pressure off capacity planning.

4. Answer: C

Explanation: Redundancy is a critical aspect of cloud infrastructure, designed to ensure that if one component (like a server or storage system) fails, there are backups ready to take over, minimizing downtime and keeping applications and data accessible at all times.

5. Answer: C

Explanation: Cloud providers enhance security by continuously monitoring their infrastructure for potential issues and proactively applying security patches and software updates. This helps to mitigate vulnerabilities and ensure that services are running on the latest and most secure versions.

6. Answer: C

Explanation: Cloud computing ensures business continuity by providing data backup, disaster recovery, and the ability to maintain critical functions after emergencies or disruptions such as security breaches, natural disasters, and power outages.

7. Answer: C

Explanation: The shared responsibility model in cloud computing outlines that while the cloud provider takes care of the underlying infrastructure, the customer is responsible for securing their applications and data within the cloud environment. This collaboration ensures a comprehensive approach to cloud security.

8. Answer: B

Explanation: Cloud providers are continually innovating, offering new features and services that allow users to access the latest advancements in technology without the need for significant investments in hardware or software upgrades.

9. Answer: B

VERSAtile Reads

Explanation: Amazon (AWS), Google (Google Cloud), and Microsoft (Azure) are the major cloud service providers that dominate the industry. They offer a broad range of services and have a significant global presence.

10. **Answer: B**

Explanation: According to the 2020 Centrify and CensusWide poll, the COVID-19 outbreak led 48% of organizations that were surveyed to accelerate their cloud migration plans to adapt to the new working conditions and digitize more of their processes.

11. **Answer: C**

Explanation: Cloud computing is based on the "Pay as you go" economic foundation, which means users only pay for the cloud services they actually utilize.

12. **Answer: B**

Explanation: In cloud computing, CapEx refers to Capital Expenditure, which is the expenditure to maintain or acquire fixed assets by spending money, such as land and equipment

13. **Answer: B**

Explanation: Cloud computing is primarily associated with Operational Expenditures (OpEx), which are the costs of running a product or system on a day-to-day basis

14. **Answer: C**

VERSAtile Reads

Explanation: The consumption-based model of cloud computing allows users to pay only for the resources they use, avoiding high upfront expenses and significant investments in infrastructure

15. Answer: C

Explanation: Elasticity in cloud computing refers to the capacity to dynamically extend or reduce network resources to respond to workload changes and optimize resource usage.

16. Answer: B

Explanation: Fault tolerance in cloud computing is the feature that ensures zero downtime by immediately mitigating any faults from the cloud provider's side

17. Answer: C

Explanation: AWS Lambda employs a consumption-based pricing model that is based on the execution of the function and resource usage.

18. Answer: C

Explanation: A main advantage of cloud computing is the automatic deployment of resources at the appropriate scale as needed, eliminating the need for manual configuration

19. Answer: C

Explanation: Software as a Service (SaaS) allows businesses to use applications without managing the underlying infrastructure, as the cloud provider handles maintenance and support

20. **Answer: A**

Explanation: Management of the Cloud involves managing cloud resources by tracking their conditions and automatically replacing failing ones, among other automated management tasks

21. **Answer: C**

Explanation: Platform as a Service (PaaS) allows users to manage the applications and services they deploy, and the cloud service provider manages the underlying server, storage, network, and database infrastructure needed for the development

22. **Answer: B**

Explanation: Infrastructure as a Service (IaaS) enables a server in the cloud or EC2 instance that you have complete control over, including the virtual machine's operating system and networking attributes

23. **Answer: C**

Explanation: Reduction in deployment time is an advantage of using PaaS, not SaaS. SaaS advantages include global access, easy access to cloud-based apps, and use of free client software

24. **Answer: B**

Explanation: The primary advantages of the public cloud deployment model are lower cost, scalability, and flexibility. You only pay for what you use and do not need to purchase and maintain expensive hardware

25. Answer: D

Explanation: Software as a Service (SaaS) is the closest to traditional on-device software but is delivered over the internet, replacing the need to install client software.

26. Answer: C

Explanation: The community cloud model allows a group of organizations to access shared infrastructure and services, offering a balance between the openness of a public cloud and the security of a private cloud

27. Answer: D

Explanation: A significant benefit of the hybrid cloud model is its ability to allow dynamic workload balancing between private and public clouds. This means organizations can seamlessly extend their infrastructure by offloading excess workloads to the public cloud during peak times while maintaining critical operations on private clouds. This dynamic balancing enhances resource utilization, ensures better performance, and provides flexibility in handling varying workloads without over-provisioning resources.

28. Answer: C

Explanation: Software as a Service (SaaS) providers handle the applications and underlying infrastructure, including software upgrades and security patches, relieving the users from managing these aspects.

29. Answer: B

Explanation: AWS is a secure cloud services platform that offers a variety of services, such as computing power, database storage, and content delivery, to help businesses scale and grow.

30. Answer: B

Explanation: The AWS Cloud Adoption Framework offers suitable advice to customers for setting up, maintaining, and introducing fresh methods using pre-existing software in their companies.

31. Answer: B

Explanation: Businesses can easily modify their computer capacity in response to demand because of AWS's unmatched scalability, which is essential for managing costs and performance.

32. Answer: A

Explanation: AWS's global network of data centers ensures low latency service access and adherence to data residency regulations.

33. Answer: C

Explanation: AWS implements robust security protocols, including identity and access control, encryption, and ongoing monitoring to protect critical data

34. Answer: C

Explanation: AWS addresses regulatory issues in various industries by adhering to various compliance requirements, ensuring that businesses can meet their legal obligations.

35. Answer: D

Explanation: AWS provides on-demand delivery of technology services via the internet with pay-as-you-go pricing, allowing users to only pay for what they use, which offers greater cost control.

36. Answer: B

Explanation: AWS allows users to experiment freely with its services without worrying about the long-term financial consequences of failed experiments.

37. Answer: B

Explanation: Serverless services in AWS allow startups with limited budgets to scale their services automatically with demand, which minimizes running costs.

38. Answer: C

Explanation: AWS allows users to provision a virtual machine that can be terminated after a short period of use, with the users only being billed for the actual time it was running, offering flexibility and cost savings.

39. Answer: B

Explanation: Companies should compare the costs and benefits of operating each workload in the cloud versus on-premises to determine the best migration approach for moving workloads to the cloud.

40. Answer: B

Explanation: Maintenance of IT equipment such as servers and air conditioners is categorized as Capital Expenditure because it enhances the equipment's usefulness and lifespan, representing an investment for future benefits.

41. Answer: C

Explanation: The AWS Well-Architected Framework provides guidelines for creating cloud architectures that are secure, reliable, efficient, and cost-optimized. This framework is integral to building successful cloud solutions on AWS.

42. Answer: C

Explanation: Automating infrastructure provisioning and configuration management ensures consistency, speed, and reduced human error. It's a best practice for achieving operational excellence on AWS.

43. Answer. B

Explanation: To protect data in transit, it is recommended to encrypt sensitive data as it moves across networks. This is a crucial aspect of maintaining security on AWS.

44. Answer: D

Explanation: Amazon EC2 Auto Scaling allows for resources to automatically adjust based on demand, which helps maintain reliability by avoiding under-provisioning and overspending.

45. **Answer: B**

Explanation: Selecting the most appropriate AWS services and resources for specific needs is essential to optimize performance and costs, ensuring performance efficiency

46. **Answer: C**

Explanation: Using services like Reserved Instances, Savings Plans, and Spot Instances can help reduce costs, aligning with the cost optimization principle of AWS cloud architecture.

47. **Answer: C**

Explanation: AWS Lambda allows for executing code without provisioning or managing servers and can be more environmentally efficient due to lower energy consumption

48. **Answer: D**

Explanation: Stateless applications can scale horizontally since no memory of previous interactions is needed, and any available computing resource can service any request

49. **Answer: C**

Explanation: Amazon RDS DB Instances can scale vertically, and the service can also scale out by adding read replicas, making it suitable for stateful components like databases

50. Answer: D

Explanation: Amazon Elastic Map Reduce (EMR) manages a fleet of EC2 instances that work on fragments of data simultaneously, making it the core service for distributed processing on AWS.

51. Answer: C

Explanation: In a cloud computing environment, treating servers as disposable resources allows for quick replacement of a server if it goes down or requires a configuration update. This approach supports rapid scaling, as servers can be launched as needed and used for as long as necessary without the need to fix or update old servers.

52. Answer: B

Explanation: Bootstrapping in the AWS cloud environment involves executing scripts after launching a resource with a default configuration, which allows for the reuse of those same scripts without modifications upon relaunching the applications.

53. Answer: C

Explanation: A golden image in AWS is a snapshot of a particular state of a resource, such as an Amazon EC2 instance or an Amazon RDS DB instance. It is used in auto-scaling to launch multiple instances with the same configurations as seen in the snapshot.

54. Answer: B

Explanation: Loose coupling is designed to minimize the reliance of components on each other, reducing the likelihood that changes in one part of the system will cause unintended changes in other parts. It helps to isolate problems and simplify testing, maintenance, and troubleshooting.

55. Answer: C

Explanation: Amazon API Gateway is the AWS service that helps developers create, publish, maintain, and monitor APIs. It manages tasks involved in accepting and processing up to thousands of concurrent API calls, such as traffic management, authorization, and access control.

56. Answer: B

Explanation: Service Discovery in a loosely coupled architecture enables services to find and interact with each other, regardless of the details of their network topology. It is essential for applications deployed as a set of smaller services that need to communicate across multiple resources.

57. Answer: C

Explanation: Technology-specific interfaces, such as RESTful APIs, allow components to interact and reduce inter-dependability. They hide the technical implementation details, enabling teams to change any underlying operations without impacting other components, which promotes loose coupling.

58. Answer: B

Explanation: Amazon's Elastic Load Balancer contributes to a loosely coupled system by using DNS endpoints to redirect requests to a copy of the database in another availability zone if, for example, the primary RDS instance goes down and Multi-AZ has been enabled. This ensures the system's resilience and availability.

59. **Answer: B**

Explanation: In asynchronous integration, an Amazon SQS Queue acts as an intermediate durable storage layer that stores messages. If a component fails while reading messages from the queue, those messages can still be added to the queue and processed once the system recovers, enhancing reliability.

60. **Answer: C**

Explanation: One of the key practices when designing architectures using AWS is to consult with AWS architects and partners for guidance and best practices. This ensures that the architecture is aligned with the latest advancements and tailored to specific business needs and objectives.

61. **Answer: C**

Explanation: Graceful failure is a design strategy that ensures that when components of an application fail, they do so without causing a significant disruption to the end-user experience. This approach helps maintain service availability and allows for offline procedures to continue, hence reducing the overall impact of failures.

62. **Answer: C**

Explanation: Best design practice for developing large-scale applications on AWS includes leveraging a wide variety of underlying technological components such as computing, storage, database, analytics, application, and deployment services. This approach enhances developer productivity and operational efficiency.

63. Answer: C

Explanation: Developers are encouraged to utilize AWS-managed services to power their applications so that they can focus more on building their applications rather than managing server infrastructure. Managed services abstract the underlying hardware and server management tasks, which simplifies maintenance and scaling.

64. Answer: B

Explanation: Amazon S3 is highly recommended for static website hosting because it can store data and scale automatically to meet traffic demands without the need for businesses to worry about technical details like capacity planning and disk configurations.

65. Answer: C

Explanation: AWS Lambda is a computing service that supports serverless architecture, allowing developers to run code without managing servers. It enables the creation of event-driven and synchronous services with reduced operational complexity.

66. Answer: D

Explanation: For customizable architectures where full control over the computing environment is desired, Amazon EC2 (Elastic Compute Cloud) is the appropriate service. It allows users to configure their virtual servers and manage all aspects of the server environment.

67. Answer: C

Explanation: Tight coupling denotes a high level of dependency between hardware and software components in a system. In a tightly coupled system, components are so interdependent that the failure of one can significantly affect the others, potentially causing the entire system to fail.

68. Answer: C

Explanation: In a tightly coupled system such as a bank ATM, the interdependence between the hardware, built-in firmware/applications, and the central banking application means that a failure in any one of these components can cause the entire system to stop functioning.

69. Answer: B

Explanation: Monolithic applications are large-scale applications where multiple related tasks and functionalities are tightly integrated into a single codebase. This tight coupling means that changes to one part of the application often require building and testing the entire application, which can be cumbersome and slow.

70. Answer: B

Explanation: The AWS Partners Program is divided into Consulting partners, who provide services like design and management of workloads on AWS, and Technology partners, who offer hardware, connectivity services, or software solutions hosted on or integrated with the AWS Cloud.

71. Answer: D

Explanation: Microservices architecture allows smaller applications to be deployed independently as loosely connected services, which can be easier to manage and update compared to a monolithic model where everything is interconnected and deployed as a single unit.

72. Answer: B

Explanation: Microservices communicate with other microservices via Application Programming Interfaces (APIs), which provide a method for passing credentials and data across applications, allowing for integrated app design.

73. Answer: C

Explanation: The six pillars of the AWS Well-Architected Framework are Operational Excellence, Security, Reliability, Performance Efficiency, Cost Optimization, and Sustainability.

74. Answer: C

Explanation: The AWS Well-Architected Tool is designed to facilitate the assessment of cloud infrastructures against AWS best practices and to help track improvements and identify high-risk issues.

75. Answer: B

Explanation: The sustainability pillar of the AWS Well-Architected Framework focuses on reducing the environmental impact of using cloud workloads.

76. Answer: B

Explanation: An AWS Region is a large area where AWS has multiple data centers. Each Region is divided into Availability Zones, which are separate, isolated locations within the Region. These Availability Zones provide redundancy and resilience, ensuring that if one zone goes down, others can still operate.

77. **Answer: B**

Explanation: The reliability pillar emphasizes that workloads should fulfill their intended functions and recover swiftly if there is a disruption, ensuring consistent reliability.

78. **Answer: C**

Explanation: The AWS Well-Architected Tool supports collaboration by allowing users to document their architecture and share it with their team, fostering greater knowledge sharing.

79. **Answer: C**

Explanation: Loose coupling in a microservices architecture means that the services are connected but not dependent on each other, which allows for individual components to fail without bringing down the entire system.

80. **Answer: B**

Explanation: The Performance Efficiency pillar is centered on the organized and efficient allocation of IT and computing resources to maintain effectiveness as company demands evolve.

81. **Answer: C**

Explanation: An Availability Zone is a data center or a collection of data centers designed with separate power, networking, and connectivity to minimize the chances of multiple zones failing at the same time. Each Availability Zone within a region is isolated to ensure high availability and fault tolerance.

82. **Answer: B**

Explanation: Edge Locations are AWS sites deployed in major cities and populated areas globally to cache data and reduce latency for end-user access. They are part of AWS's Content Delivery Network (CDN) and help in delivering content with reduced latency.

83. **Answer: B**

Explanation: AWS has deployed more than 102 Edge Locations around the world, which are used to cache data and provide content to users with reduced latency.

84. **Answer: C**

Explanation: A Regional Edge Cache is a new type of edge location that sits between CloudFront origin servers and edge locations. It retains expired data so that if an edge location experiences a cache miss, it can retrieve the cached data from the Regional Edge Cache instead of the origin servers, which reduces latency.

85. **Answer: B**

Explanation: AWS Global Accelerator is a service that improves the availability and performance of applications for local and global users by directing traffic over the AWS global network.

86. Answer: C

Explanation: For a standard accelerator in AWS Global Accelerator, the endpoints can include Network Load Balancers, Application Load Balancers, Amazon EC2 instances, and Elastic IP addresses.

87. Answer: C

Explanation: AWS Global Accelerator enhances internet user performance by up to 60% by routing user traffic through the Amazon backbone network, which helps maintain consistent packet loss, jitter, and latency even when the internet is congested.

88. Answer: A

Explanation: AWS Global Accelerator provides two static IP addresses that act as a single fixed entry point for your clients, facilitating traffic management and enabling seamless addition or removal of AWS resources from the backend without impacting the customer interface.

89. Answer: D

Explanation: AWS's Global Infrastructure includes 25 geographic regions, 81 availability zones, and a network of edge locations, but it does not include dedicated physical stores for consumers as it is a cloud-based infrastructure service.

90. Answer: B

Explanation: BYOIP stands for Bring Your Own IP address range. In the context of AWS Global Accelerator, it allows you to use your IP address range with Global Accelerator, or you can opt to use static IP addresses from your pool with your accelerator.

91. Answer: C

Explanation: AWS Outposts are designed to extend AWS's infrastructure, services, and tools to on-premises facilities. They are beneficial for workloads that need to remain on-premises due to low latency requirements, local data processing needs, or specific regulatory compliance.

92. Answer: A

Explanation: AWS Outposts provide access to a subset of AWS services that can be run locally, including EC2, EBS, ECS, RDS, and others, offering a consistent hybrid experience

93. Answer: B

Explanation: AWS Local Zones are primarily used to provide low latency services in specific geographic areas. They extend AWS services closer to end-users, which helps reduce latency for applications that require single-digit millisecond latencies. This is particularly beneficial for applications like gaming, media, and entertainment content creation, real-time simulations, and machine learning inference.

94. Answer: B

Explanation: AWS Wavelength brings AWS compute and storage services to the edge of 5G networks by integrating AWS services into the telecommunications providers' data centers, enabling ultra-low latency applications.

95. Answer: A

Explanation: AWS Systems Manager gives visibility and control over AWS resources, allowing users to automate operational tasks monitor, and troubleshoot AWS infrastructure.

96. Answer: D

Explanation: AWS Systems Manager features include patch and session management and automated resource grouping, but it is not a service for web hosting.

97. Answer: C

Explanation: SSM Agent, installed on managed nodes, is responsible for making the configuration changes or operations on resources as requested through AWS Systems Manager.

98. Answer: B

Explanation: AWS Wavelength is ideal for applications that require ultra-low latencies, such as real-time analytics, because it operates at the edge of 5G networks within telecom providers' data centers.

99. Answer: D

Explanation: All of the above options support edge computing scenarios by bringing AWS services closer to end-users or devices – AWS Outposts through on-premises deployment, AWS Local Zones through geographical proximity, and AWS Wavelength through integration with 5G networks.

100. Answer: C

Explanation: In AWS Systems Manager, a managed node refers to a computing resource that can be managed via the service. This includes Amazon EC2 instances, edge devices, on-premises servers, and virtual machines, including those in other cloud environments.

101. Answer: B

Explanation: Each object in Amazon S3 can contain up to 5 TB of data. This allows users to store large files as a single object within an S3 bucket.

102. Answer: B

Explanation: Amazon S3 bucket names are globally unique, regardless of the AWS Region in which you create the bucket, ensuring that each bucket can be uniquely accessed across the world.

103. Answer: C

Explanation: Amazon Simple Storage Service (Amazon S3) is an object storage service that provides a simple web service interface to store and retrieve any type and amount of data.

104. Answer: C

Explanation: All new Amazon S3 buckets are private by default, with no public read access. Bucket policies can be modified if public access is required, for example, to host a static website.

105. Answer: A

Explanation: Amazon S3 is not suitable for hosting dynamic websites that require a database connection. It is designed to host static websites, such as .html pages.

106. Answer: C

Explanation: The key of an object in an S3 bucket acts as the unique identifier for the object within that bucket, similar to a name.

107. Answer: B

Explanation: Choosing an AWS Region that is geographically close to you can help optimize latency and minimize costs when creating an Amazon S3 bucket.

108. Answers: B

Explanation: Amazon S3 Standard provides a durability of 99.999999999% (11 nines) for objects stored, but when it comes to availability, it offers a guarantee of 99.99%.

109. Answer: D

Explanation: Amazon S3 allows for concurrent read and write access to data by many separate clients or application threads, which is a part of its scalable storage solution.

110. Answer: C

Explanation: Bucket policies and access control lists (ACLs) are used to manage object permissions in Amazon S3, controlling who can access your data.

111. Answer: D

Explanation: Reduced Redundancy Storage (RRS) is designed for non-critical, reproducible data that doesn't require the same level of redundancy as the other storage classes.

112. Answer: A

Explanation: Cross Region Replication (CRR) allows you to automatically replicate the contents of one S3 bucket to another bucket located in a different AWS Region.

113. Answer: C

Explanation: If a file is successfully uploaded to an S3 bucket, an HTTP 200 status code is returned to indicate success.

114. Answer: B

Explanation: Amazon S3 provides Read after Write consistency for PUTS of new objects, meaning that as soon as a new object is written, it can be immediately read

115. Answer: B

Explanation: S3 Standard-IA (Infrequent Access) is ideal for data that isn't accessed often but requires quick access when it is needed, such as for long-term backups or disaster recovery.

116. Answer: B

Explanation: The minimum object size for S3 Standard-IA and S3 One Zone-IA is 128 KB. Objects smaller than this size may not be cost-effective in these storage classes due to minimum billing sizes.

117. Answer: C

Explanation: Query String Authentication is used to share S3 objects via URLs that are valid only for a specified limited period.

118. Answer: B

Explanation: Amazon S3 Access Points simplify access management for shared datasets in S3 by providing customized endpoints with fine-grained access control policies, ensuring scalability, security, and simplified management.

119. Answer: D

Explanation: AWS Backup is a fully managed service designed to simplify the protection of your data across AWS services in the cloud and on-premises. It allows for the central management of backup policies and monitoring of backup activity.

120. Answer: B

Explanation: In AWS services, the term "recovery point" is used synonymously with "backup." A recovery point is a snapshot of the content of a resource at a specific point in time.

121. Answer: A

Explanation: AWS Backup stores its recovery points in Amazon S3 buckets. Amazon S3 (Simple Storage Service) is a highly durable and scalable object storage service provided by Amazon Web Services. AWS Backup leverages S3 to store backup data securely and durably.

122. Answer: D

Explanation: Amazon Glacier is a low-cost storage service optimized for infrequently accessed data, making it ideal for long-term archiving and backup.

123. Answer: B

Explanation: Amazon Glacier is designed for data that does not require immediate availability, with retrieval times typically ranging from 3 to 5 hours

124. Answer: D

Explanation: AWS Storage Gateway is a service that connects an on-premises software appliance with cloud-based storage, providing a secure and seamless bridge between an organization's IT environment and AWS's storage infrastructure.

125. Answer: B

Explanation: The Vault Lock feature in Amazon Glacier allows enforcement of compliance requirements by using a lockable policy that is designed for Write Once Read Many (WORM) storage.

126. Answer: C

Explanation: AWS Backup helps maintain an organization's data protection policies and regulatory compliance by providing a centralized platform to manage backup settings and monitor activity.

127. Answer: C

Explanation: Amazon Glacier has a minimum storage duration of 90 days, making it suitable for long-term data retention.

128. Answer: B

Explanation: Each volume in Volume Gateway Stored Mode supports a maximum of 16TB. A single gateway can support up to 32 volumes, leading to a maximum storage of 512TB, but the size limit for a single volume is 16TB.

129. Answer: B

Explanation: In Volume Gateway Cached Mode, a single gateway can support up to 32 volumes, allowing for significant scaling of storage capacity within the cloud.

130. Answer: C

Explanation: Each volume in Volume Gateway Cached Mode can support up to 32TB, and with the gateway supporting 32 volumes, the maximum storage capacity per gateway reaches 1PB.

131. Answer: D

Explanation: Amazon Aurora is a relational database compatible with MySQL and PostgreSQL and is designed to handle complex transactions and support JOIN operations. It is a fully managed service that offers the speed and reliability of high-end commercial databases with the simplicity and cost-effectiveness of open-source databases.

132. Answer: B

Explanation: Amazon DynamoDB is a NoSQL database service that automatically scales horizontally through data partitioning and replication. It is designed to handle large-scale, high-availability applications with seamless scalability and fast performance.

133. Answer: D

Explanation: Amazon Redshift is a data warehouse service that is optimized for analytics and reporting of large datasets. It uses massive parallel processing, columnar data storage, and targeted data compression encoding to achieve efficient storage and optimum query performance.

134. Answer: B

Explanation: Amazon ES, or Amazon ElasticSearch Service, offers an open-source API that allows users more control over the configuration details compared to Amazon CloudSearch, which is a more managed search service with less configuration required.

135. Answer: B

Explanation: Amazon Neptune achieves high availability by synchronously replicating the database volume across three Availability Zones within a single AWS region, ensuring fault tolerance and data durability.

136. Answer: C

Explanation: Amazon Neptune is a graph database designed specifically to store and navigate relationships, making it ideal for use cases such as social networking, recommendation engines, and fraud detection.

137. Answer: C

Explanation: Amazon ElastiCache is an AWS service that makes it easy to deploy, operate, and scale an in-memory cache in the cloud, which can significantly improve application performance by providing a high-speed data storage layer.

138. Answer: C

Explanation: Amazon RDS Multi-AZ deployments are designed to provide high availability by automatically failing over to a standby replica in another Availability Zone in case of an outage, maintenance, or failure of the primary instance.

139. Answer: C

Explanation: Amazon DynamoDB's Time-to-live (TTL) feature allows you to define a specific timestamp to automatically delete expired items from your tables, thus saving space and potentially reducing costs.

140. Answer: C

Explanation: AWS-managed services like Amazon RDS and Amazon DynamoDB offload the administrative burdens of running and scaling a database, including tasks such as hardware provisioning, software patching, setup, configuration, and backups, allowing you to focus on application development

141. Answer: B

Explanation: Amazon FSx for Windows File Server is designed to provide a fully managed native Microsoft Windows file system, which allows easy migration of Windows-based applications that require file storage to AWS.

142. Answer: D

Explanation: Elastic File System (EFS) is Linux-based only and does not support connections from EC2 instances running Windows. Instead, EFS is used for Linux instances and Linux-based applications.

143. Answer: D

Explanation: Amazon FSx for Lustre is optimized for compute-intensive workloads, such as High-Performance Computing (HPC), Machine Learning, Media Data Processing of workflow, and Electronic Design Automation (EDA).

144. Answer: D

Explanation: Amazon FSx for Windows is specifically used for Windows-based applications such as SharePoint, Microsoft SQL Server, Workspace (Internet Information Services), IIS Web Server, or any other Microsoft application, while EFS is used for Linux instances and applications.

145. Answer: D

Explanation: AWS Elastic Disaster Recovery (AWS DRS) allows you to run non-disruptive tests to ensure that the disaster recovery implementation is complete and maintain readiness during normal operations.

146. Answer: C

Explanation: AWS Snowcone is designed as a lightweight, reliable, and secure device for data transport and edge computing, suitable for use in environments with limited space or inconsistent network connectivity.

147. Answer: C

Explanation: Snowcone SSD is the version of AWS Snowcone that includes 14 TB of solid-state drive (SSD)-based storage, along with two virtual CPUs and 4 GB of RAM.

148. Answer: C

Explanation: Amazon FSx for Lustre can store data directly to Amazon S3, making it suitable for applications that need high-speed, high-capacity distributed storage

149. Answer: B

Explanation: A Snowcone device can operate on battery power for up to about 6 hours with a light workload, which involves 25% CPU usage, allowing for mobile deployments.

150. Answer: B

Explanation: Snowcone devices provide a file interface with Network File System (NFS) capability, enabling data transfer from local Windows, Linux, and macOS servers and file-based applications.

151. Answer: C

Explanation: IAM is a web service that helps you securely control access to AWS resources. Users can manage authentication and authorization, controlling who is signed in and what permissions they have to use AWS resources.

152. Answer: C

Explanation: The AWS account root user has full access to all AWS services and resources. It is recommended to use this account only to create other IAM user accounts and to secure it with multi-factor authentication due to its extensive privileges.

153. Answer: C

Explanation: An IAM User is a unique identity within an AWS account and can represent a person, system, or application. These users have limited access as defined by their IAM permissions and policies.

154. Answer: C

Explanation: An IAM Group is a collection of IAM users. You can specify permissions for multiple users by managing the group's permissions, making it easier to handle permissions for all users within the group.

155. Answer: C

Explanation: IAM Roles offer a secure way to delegate permissions that do not require long-term credentials. This means that roles can provide temporary security credentials for the user or service that assumes the role, which are automatically rotated and have a configurable expiration time.

156. Answer: C

Explanation: IAM resources, including users, groups, and roles, are universal and not tied to any specific AWS region. This means that they can be used across different regions without the need for duplication.

157. Answer: C

Explanation: By default, IAM users, groups, and roles have no permissions. Permissions must be explicitly granted through policies.

158. Answer: D

Explanation: IAM policies can be applied in several ways, including attaching a managed policy, attaching an inline policy, or adding the user to a group that already has appropriate permission policies attached.

159. Answer: B

Explanation: IAM Groups cannot be nested within other groups. A group can contain multiple IAM users, and a user can belong to multiple groups. Still, groups can only be used to manage permissions and do not have any security credentials of their own.

160. Answer: C

Explanation: An IAM Role is used to delegate access within or between AWS accounts. It allows you to define a set of permissions for making AWS service requests without attaching these permissions to a specific IAM user or group.

161. Answer: B

Explanation: A VPC endpoint allows a Virtual Private Cloud (VPC) to privately connect to AWS services without the need for an internet gateway, NAT device, VPN connection, or AWS Direct Connect. It ensures that the traffic between the VPC and AWS services does not leave the Amazon network.

162. Answer: C

Explanation: AWS offers two types of VPC endpoints: Interface endpoints and Gateway endpoints. Interface endpoints enable private connections to services using PrivateLink, whereas Gateway endpoints are used as a target for route tables to route traffic directly to Amazon S3 and DynamoDB.

163. Answer: B

Explanation: Amazon S3 and DynamoDB are the two services that are supported by Gateway endpoints in AWS. This enables private connections from the VPC to these services without the need to traverse the public internet.

164. Answer: C

Explanation: Interface endpoints use security groups to control the traffic to and from the service to which it is connected. This provides a secure method of communication between the VPC and the supported AWS services.

165. Answer: C

Explanation: AWS PrivateLink is utilized within Interface endpoints to access AWS services privately using private IP addresses. This service ensures that all traffic is restricted to the Amazon network, thereby enhancing security and privacy.

166. Answer: B

Explanation: VPC peering cannot be established between VPCs that have matching or overlapping CIDR blocks. This is because each VPC in a peering connection must have a unique IP address range.

167. Answer: B

Explanation: An AWS Managed VPN provides a secure, tunneled connection over the internet using IPSec encryption, which is redundant and can serve as a backup for Direct Connect or another VPN link.

168. Answer: A

Explanation: AWS Direct Connect allows for the establishment of a private, logical connection from a remote network to an Amazon VPC, offering predictable network performance with potential cost reductions in bandwidth.

169. Answer: C

Explanation: An Application Load Balancer makes routing decisions at the application layer (Layer 7), which is ideal for advanced routing capabilities and applications that require content-based routing.

170. Answer: A

Explanation: A Classic Load Balancer is the right choice when you need simple load balancing of traffic across multiple EC2 instances and your application is built within the EC2-Classic network or a VPC. It routes traffic based on application or network-level information.

171. Answer: B

Explanation: MFA adds a layer of security by requiring a second form of authentication in addition to the username and password. This ensures that account access is more secure against unauthorized use.

172. Answer: D

Explanation: The supported MFA methods are Virtual MFA Devices, U2F Security Key, and Hardware MFA devices. SMS-based verification is not mentioned as a supported method for AWS MFA.

173. Answer: C

Explanation: With MFA enabled, IAM users are required to submit unique authentication from an AWS-supported MFA method in addition to their regular sign-in credentials.

174. Answer: C

Explanation: A virtual MFA device generates a six-digit numeric code that users must enter during sign-in as part of the authentication process.

175. Answer: C

Explanation: The difference is in the interaction; a U2F Security Key needs the user to touch the device for authentication, while a Hardware MFA device traditionally requires a code to be entered manually.

176. Answer: B

Explanation: Users of AWS SSO can set up MFA using two different authenticator applications simultaneously, offering redundancy and flexibility in generating MFA codes for login.

177. Answer: A

Explanation: TouchID on a MacBook is given as an example of a FIDO2-enabled built-in authenticator that can be used as a valid second factor for MFA.

178. Answer: B

Explanation: FIDO2 and WebAuthn protect user privacy by creating unique cryptographic data for each site, and when biometrics are used, that data does not leave the user's device.

179. Answer: B

Explanation: If users have compatibility issues with their U2F devices, it is advised to contact the device provider for potential solutions or to determine if they are using an unsupported browser.

180. Answer: A

Explanation: Users can utilize third-party authenticator applications as approved MFA devices on AWS if they support RFC 6238, which is a standards-based TOTP algorithm capable of generating six-digit authentication codes.

181. Answer: C

Explanation: Amazon CloudFront is a global Content Delivery Network (CDN) service that securely delivers data, videos, applications, and APIs to users with low latency and high transfer speeds.

182. Answer: C

Explanation: The origins of Amazon CloudFront can be an Amazon S3 bucket, an EC2 instance, an Elastic Load Balancer, or an HTTP server. Amazon DynamoDB is not listed as an origin type for CloudFront.

183. Answer: B

Explanation: Regional edge caches have a larger cache width than any individual edge location, meaning objects remain in the cache longer at the nearest regional edge caches, reducing the need to return to the origin web server.

184. Answer: C

Explanation: Amazon CloudFront routes the user's request to the nearest CloudFront edge location that best serves the request in terms of latency, and if the content is in the cache, it is delivered immediately.

185. Answer: C

Explanation: In CloudFront, a distribution is the name given to the CDN, which consists of a collection of edge locations.

186. Answer: B

Explanation: Amazon CloudFront is seamlessly integrated with AWS WAF and AWS Shield Advanced to protect your applications from sophisticated threats.

187. Answer: C

Explanation: Lambda@Edge allows you to run your code across AWS locations worldwide, enabling you to respond to your end-users with the lowest latency.

188. Answer: B

Explanation: CloudFront is directly connected with hundreds of end-user ISPs, which accelerates the delivery of end-to-end content.

189. Answer: D

Explanation: Amazon CloudFront has no long-term contracts or minimum monthly usage commitments. You pay only for as much or as little content as you deliver through the service.

190. Answer: D

Explanation: Amazon CloudFront is optimized to work with Amazon S3, EC2, Elastic Load Balancing, and Amazon Route 53, but it does not have a deep integration with Amazon RDS

191. Answer: C

Explanation: Amazon Route 53 is a scalable and highly available Cloud DNS web service designed to connect user requests to infrastructure running in AWS, such as EC2 instances, Elastic Load Balancers, or Amazon S3 buckets, as well as to infrastructure outside of AWS.

192. Answer: D

Explanation: DNS, or Domain Name System, translates human-readable domain names like www.example.com to numeric IP addresses like 192.0.2.1, which are used by computers to connect.

193. Answer: D

Explanation: Amazon Route 53 supports various routing types, including latency-based routing, Geo DNS, and weighted round-robin, but it does not support direct server return routing.

194. Answer: A

Explanation: DNS Failover can be combined with Route 53's various routing types to manage traffic enabling low-latency and fault-tolerant architectures.

195. Answer: D

Explanation: Although Elastic Compute Cloud (EC2) instances can be routed using Route 53, the service itself is primarily focused on DNS Management, Traffic Management, and Availability Monitoring and is not a compute service like Elastic Compute Cloud (EC2).

196. Answer: C

Explanation: A bastion host is a special-purpose server that serves as the primary access point from the Internet and acts as a proxy for other EC2 instances.

197. Answer: B

Explanation: A bastion host is usually positioned on the outside of a firewall or in a Demilitarized Zone (DMZ) to provide access from untrusted networks or computers.

198. Answer: B

Explanation: NAT Gateway offers better availability, higher bandwidth, and requires less administration than NAT instances.

199. Answer: B

Explanation: NAT instances and gateways enable instances within a private subnet in a VPC to access the internet for tasks such as downloading patches or updating software.

200. Answer: B

Explanation: Because the bastion host acts as a bridge to private instances and is exposed to potential attacks, it should be hardened to enhance security.

201. Answer: D

Explanation: AWS Cloud Map is a service discovery and resource location tracking tool that allows applications to find the most current locations of their resources, thereby increasing the availability of the application.

202. Answer: D

Explanation: AWS Cloud Map increases application availability by continuously monitoring the health of IP-based components and dynamically updating the location of each microservice as it is added or withdrawn, ensuring applications always find the most current resource location.

203. Answer: B

Explanation: AWS Cloud Map boosts developer productivity by offering a single registry where unique names for all application services can be specified, reducing the need to continuously track, save, and update resource names and locations or make changes to the application code.

204. Answer: B

Explanation: AWS Network Firewall is a stateful, managed network firewall and intrusion detection and prevention service that filters traffic at the periphery of a virtual private cloud (VPC).

205. Answer: C

Explanation: AWS Network Firewall uses Suricata, an open-source intrusion prevention system (IPS) for stateful inspection of network traffic.

206. Answer: A

Explanation: AWS Network Firewall offers both stateless and stateful rules for filtering traffic. Stateless rules assess individual packets based on predefined criteria, while stateful rules consider the context of network connections, providing more sophisticated filtering capabilities.

207. Answer: C

Explanation: AWS Network Firewall integrates with AWS Organizations through AWS Firewall Manager, which allows centralized configuration and management of firewalls across all accounts and applications.

208. Answer: A

Explanation: AWS-managed database services support various database engines, including relational and NoSQL databases.

209. Answer: B

Explanation: The Amazon RDS Multi-AZ deployment feature ensures high availability by creating a synchronously replicated standby instance in a different Availability Zone, allowing automatic switchover in case of primary node failure.

210. Answer: B

Explanation: A NoSQL database should be considered when an application does not require the features of joins or complex transactions that are typical in relational databases.

211. Answer: B

Explanation: Amazon Simple Queue Service (SQS) is designed to help developers decouple and scale their microservices, distributed systems, and serverless applications efficiently. It is a managed message queuing service that removes the complexity and operational overhead associated with message-oriented middleware.

212. Answer: C

Explanation: FIFO stands for First In First Out. This is the order in which messages are processed in Amazon SQS, meaning the first message sent to the queue is the first one to be received and processed.

213. Answer: C

Explanation: FIFO queues in Amazon SQS offer exactly one message processing, which ensures that each message is delivered and processed only one time, eliminating the possibility of duplicate processing.

214. Answer: C

Explanation: Amazon SQS ensures high message durability by saving messages on multiple servers. This redundant storage strategy protects against message loss if hardware failures occur.

215. Answer: A

Explanation: The maximum size of a message that Amazon SQS can handle directly is 256 KB. For larger messages, Amazon SQS can reference an Amazon S3 object, or the message can be divided into smaller parts.

216. Answer: A

Explanation: Amazon SQS uses Server-Side Encryption (SSE) to secure the transmission of sensitive data, which encrypts the contents of queued messages with keys managed by AWS Key Management Service (AWS KMS).

217. Answer: A

Explanation: Amazon SQS is a cloud-based service and does not support on-premises deployment. It is designed to be highly scalable, reliable, and available, operating with redundant infrastructure to ensure message accessibility.

218. Answer: C

Explanation: Amazon SQS can scale transparently to handle demand surges or spikes by processing each delayed request individually without the need for any manual provisioning instructions.

219. Answer: B

Explanation: To handle messages larger than 256 KB, Amazon SQS can be used in conjunction with Amazon Simple Storage Service (Amazon S3), which can store the contents of large messages, with SQS referencing the Amazon S3 object.

220. Answer: C

Explanation: For new applications that demand nearly unlimited scalability and simple APIs, Amazon SQS and Amazon SNS are recommended. They are highly scalable services that do not require the setup of message brokers.

221. Answer: D

Explanation: AWS DocumentDB is designed to be compatible with MongoDB, allowing users to utilize it as a managed MongoDB database on AWS. It is a MongoDB drop-in solution, meaning it can interface with AWS services just like MongoDB, with only a few minor differences.

222. Answer: C

Explanation: AWS DocumentDB has storage auto-scaling features, but it only scales upwards, similar to the Aurora storage engine. It does not scale downwards automatically. It also supports automatic failover to replicas and can index JSON data structures.

223. Answer: B

Explanation: One of the use cases for AWS DocumentDB is storing social media profiles because they consist of semi-static attributes that fit well within a document store database. It is not ideal for high-frequency stock trading or real-time applications where transactional systems are required.

224. Answer: B

Explanation: Amazon ElastiCache is compatible with two widely used caching engines: Redis and Memcached. It offers a managed in-memory data store or cache for these engines, providing high performance and low latency.

225. Answer: C

Explanation: ElastiCache Auto-Discovery for Memcached allows applications to automatically discover and connect to all the nodes in a cache cluster. This eliminates the need for manual tracking of hostnames and port numbers and ensures applications adapt to changes in cluster node membership.

226. Answer: D

Explanation: Among the features provided by AWS ElastiCache that improve the reliability of production deployments is the automatic detection and recovery of node failures. This ensures that the cache environment remains stable and available even if individual nodes encounter problems.

227. Answer: C

Explanation: In ElastiCache for Redis, a cluster is the cornerstone structure. It consists of one or more cache nodes, each running an instance of the Redis cache engine. Clusters can be managed using the AWS CLI, ElastiCache API, or AWS Management Console.

228. Answer: C

Explanation: Running an ElastiCache cluster in an Amazon VPC provides complete control over the virtual networking environment, including the IP address range, subnets, routing, and access control lists. It enhances the security and isolation of the cache cluster.

229. Answer: B

Explanation: A Multi-AZ deployment in AWS is designed to provide data redundancy and failover capabilities. It involves creating a primary node instance and a backup standby instance in separate Availability Zones, ensuring continuity and stability of the service in case of failures.

230. Answer: D

Explanation: Amazon CloudWatch is used to monitor the performance and health of an ElastiCache for the Redis cluster. It provides metrics and alarms that can be utilized to keep track of the system's status and send notifications of any significant changes or issues.

231. Answer: C

Explanation: Amazon Database Migration Service (DMS) helps in migrating on-premises databases to AWS Cloud. It supports continuous replication with minimal downtime, making it the primary service for database migration.

232. Answer: B

Explanation: AWS Schema Conversion Tool (AWS SCT) is used to convert database schemas from one database engine to another as part of the migration process, making it possible to switch database engines during migration.

233. Answer: B

Explanation: AWS Server Migration Service (SMS) is designed to automate the migration of on-premises server VMs to AWS Cloud by creating Amazon Machine Images (AMIs) that can be deployed on Amazon EC2 instances.

234. Answer: C

Explanation: AWS DataSync speeds up online data transfers significantly. It is designed to be faster and more automated compared to open-source tools, offering up to 10 times the transfer speed.

235. Answer: C

Explanation: Amazon Redshift is AWS's fully managed, scalable data warehousing solution that allows for querying and analyzing large data sets efficiently.

236. Answer: B

Explanation: AWS Snowball is a physical device that acts like a giant disk. It is used to transfer large amounts of data by shipping the device with the data to AWS, making it an efficient solution for transferring substantial amounts of data.

237. Answer: B

Explanation: The primary feature that distinguishes Amazon Elastic File System (EFS) from Amazon Elastic Block Store (EBS) is its elasticity. EFS automatically adjusts its size as files are added or removed.

VERSAtile Reads

238. Answer: C

Explanation: AWS CodeDeploy is used to deploy application code to various targets, including EC2 instances and on-premises servers, making it a versatile solution for code deployment across environments.

239. Answer: B

Explanation: AWS Server Migration Service (SMS) manages multi-server migrations by allowing the scheduling of replications and tracking the status of servers that are part of an application.

240. Answer: B

Explanation: The AWS Storage Gateway is a hybrid cloud service that is typically used to cache files on-premises and seamlessly replicate them to Amazon S3, providing an efficient bridge between on-premises environments and AWS Cloud storage.

241. Answer: C

Explanation: AWS PrivateLink is designed to connect services within a VPC to other VPCs using private IP addresses. This ensures secure access to AWS services and endpoint services hosted by other AWS accounts without exposing the traffic to the public internet. It uses elastic network interfaces with IP addresses from the VPC's subnets, allowing the use of VPC Security Groups to control access.

242. Answer: C

Explanation: AWS Transit Gateway is designed for a hub-and-spoke network topology, allowing customers to connect thousands of VPCs and on-premises networks. It simplifies management and reduces operating costs compared to other connectivity methods like VPC peering, which is not scalable for thousands of connections.

243. Answer: B

Explanation: A Network Load Balancer is required on the service VPC for AWS PrivateLink to function. It allows the service VPC application to connect to the Network Load Balancer, which in turn can be exposed to customer VPCs via AWS PrivateLink, using Elastic Network Interfaces on the customer side.

244. Answer: C

Explanation: You can connect to up to three Transit Gateways at a time for hybrid connectivity via a single Direct Connect Connection. This limitation is important to consider when designing your network architecture for connecting AWS resources to on-premises networks.

245. Answer: C

Explanation: AWS Transit Gateway abstracts away the complexity of managing individual VPN connections and eliminates the need for managing EC2-based software appliances for traffic routing. AWS handles the resources required for traffic routing, providing a highly available and scalable solution.

246. Answer: B

Explanation: AWS App Mesh is the managed version of Service Mesh offered by AWS, designed for monitoring and managing communications between microservices running on AWS. It allows for end-to-end visibility and traffic control to ensure the high availability of microservices.

247. Answer: B

Explanation: In AWS App Mesh, a Virtual Node represents the combination of a deployment and a service. It requires a DNS endpoint for connection and is identified by a name that must match an environment variable in the Envoy proxy for recognition. Virtual Nodes define which services they can access and how they can be accessed.

248. Answer: C

Explanation: AWS Transit Gateway uses route tables to control traffic flow among all the connected spoke networks, which includes VPCs and on-premises networks. This mechanism simplifies network management and allows for the separation of routing domains when necessary.

249. Answer: C

Explanation: AWS Transit Gateway provides improved bandwidth for inter-VPC communication, allowing for burst speeds of up to 50 Gbps per Availability Zone. This bandwidth improvement enhances performance for high-volume traffic scenarios.

250. Answer: C

Explanation: AWS App Mesh simplifies the management of service-to-service communication in microservices architectures. It provides a dedicated infrastructure layer that manages service communication, ensuring reliable and secure interactions between different components of an application.

251. Answer: C

Explanation: AWS is responsible for protecting the infrastructure that runs all of the services offered in the AWS Cloud. This infrastructure includes the hardware, software, networking, and facilities that run AWS Cloud services.

252. Answer: C

Explanation: AWS Artifact offers access to a range of compliance documentation and reports that help customers understand AWS security and compliance capabilities.

253. Answer: B

Explanation: While AWS is PCI DSS compliant up to the infrastructure layer, customers are responsible for ensuring their specific implementations are compliant, which may require additional gap audits and security measures.

254. Answer: B

Explanation: HIPAA/HITECH standards are specifically designed to protect sensitive patient healthcare information and are applicable to entities dealing with healthcare data.

255. Answer: C

Explanation: For managed services, AWS handles basic security tasks such as the guest operating system and database patching, firewall configuration, and disaster recovery.

256. Answer: C

Explanation: PCI DSS Level 1 is the Payment Card Industry Data Security Standard for entities that handle online payments and involves storing, processing, or transmitting cardholder data.

257. Answer: C

Explanation: ISO 27001 is a widely-recognized certification that provides a set of standardized requirements for an Information Security Management System (ISMS), ensuring best practices in security management.

258. Answer: A

Explanation: Users can access AWS Artifact to view and download compliance reports by logging into the AWS Management Console and finding AWS Artifact in the "Security, Identity, & Compliance" section.

259. Answer: C

Explanation: AWS's adherence to a broad set of compliance programs and certifications enables customers to meet compliance requirements for a multitude of regulatory agencies worldwide.

260. Answer: C

Explanation: While AWS secures the cloud infrastructure, security within the cloud – including protecting customer data, managing access controls, and configuring network protections – is the responsibility of the customer.

261. Answer: B

Explanation: AWS Shield is a managed protection service that safeguards web applications running on AWS against Distributed Denial-of-Service (DDoS) attacks.

262. Answer: B

Explanation: AWS Shield offers two tiers:

- AWS Shield Standard: Included for all AWS customers at no extra cost, providing basic protection against common DDoS attacks.
- AWS Shield Advanced: An optional paid service with advanced features, such as 24/7 DDoS response, cost protection, and integration with AWS WAF, priced at $3,000 per month.

263. Answer: C

Explanation: AWS Shield Standard protects against more commonly occurring Infrastructure (OSI layer 3 and layer 4) attacks such as SYN/UDP Floods, Reflection attacks, and others.

264. Answer: B

Explanation: AWS Shield Advanced delivers enhanced protection against more significant and more sophisticated attacks through the flow-based monitoring of network traffic.

265. Answer: C

Explanation: AWS Shield Advanced is an optional paid service priced at $3,000 per month. It provides enhanced DDoS protection with access to the AWS DDoS Response Team, cost protection features, advanced attack analytics, integration with AWS WAF, and DDoS cost protection.

266. Answer: C

Explanation: AWS Shield Advanced is accessible to AWS Business Support and AWS Enterprise Support customers.

267. Answer: C

Explanation: AWS Shield Standard is a DDoS protection service provided by AWS at no extra cost to all customers. It automatically defends against common DDoS attacks, offers global protection, and provides visibility and reporting features.

268. Answer: B

Explanation: The purpose of AWS Shield is to safeguard web applications running on AWS with always-on detection and automatic inline mitigations against DDoS attacks.

269. Answer: B

Explanation: A Distributed Denial-of-Service (DDoS) attack is a malicious attempt to disrupt the availability of a targeted system by flooding it with packets or requests.

270. Answer: B

Explanation: AWS Shield Standard is designed to maintain the high availability of applications on AWS by protecting against common infrastructure attacks.

271. Answer: C

Explanation: AWS CloudWatch is primarily used to monitor the performance of AWS resources and the applications running on AWS. It provides metrics such as CPU utilization, network utilization, disk utilization, and custom metrics like RAM utilization and the status of EC2 instances.

272. Answer: A

Explanation: AWS Config provides a detailed view of the configuration of AWS resources in an AWS account, including how resources are related and how configurations change over time. It's used for compliance auditing, security analysis, change management, and operational troubleshooting.

273. Answer: C

Explanation: Penetration testing, also known as pentest, can be carried out without prior approval for eight AWS services, including EC2, RDS, Aurora, and Lambda.

274. Answer: B

Explanation: AWS KMS (Key Management Service) is a multi-tenant service that manages cryptographic keys, whereas AWS CloudHSM is a single-tenant service that provides hardware security modules for key management and is compliant with FIPS 140-2 level 3.

275. Answer: B

Explanation: AWS Secrets Manager helps protect access to applications, services, and IT resources by managing and rotating secrets like database credentials and API keys throughout their lifecycle. It also supports automatic secret rotations and integration with RDS.

276. Answer: C

Explanation AWS Control Tower is used for setting up and governing a secure, multi-account AWS environment efficiently. It allows the provisioning of multiple AWS accounts that adhere to company policies.

277. Answer: C

Explanation: Amazon GuardDuty is a threat detection service that continuously monitors for malicious activity and unauthorized behavior, protecting AWS accounts, workloads, and data stored in Amazon S3.

278. Answer: C

Explanation: Compromised IAM credentials, such as those inadvertently shared on GitHub, need to be invalidated and replaced manually. This involves determining the extent of access, suspending the credentials, and reviewing access to the AWS account.

279. Answer: D

Explanation: The AWS Glue Data Catalog acts as a central schema repository and is part of AWS Glue, a fully managed ETL (Extract, Transform, and Load) service that facilitates the movement and transformation of data across different data stores.

280. Answer: B

Explanation: AWS Parameter Store is a free service that can store up to 10,000 parameters, and it can be used for storing configuration data and secrets. AWS Secrets Manager does everything Parameter Store does but without the parameter limit; however, it is a paid service.

281. Answer: D

Explanation: The primary purpose of Amazon Athena is to analyze data in S3 using standard SQL. Athena is an interactive query service that allows users to query structured, semi-structured, and unstructured data stored in Amazon S3 using familiar SQL syntax without the need for server provisioning or management.

282. Answer: C

Explanation: XML. Amazon Athena supports a variety of data formats, such as CSV, TSV, JSON, Textfiles, ORC, and Parquet. However, XML is not listed as one of the supported data formats.

283. Answer: B

Explanation: Amazon Macie is primarily used for the automatic detection, classification, and protection of sensitive data in AWS. Macie leverages machine learning and pattern matching to identify and secure PII and other sensitive information stored in AWS, particularly within S3 buckets.

284. Answer: B

Explanation: AWS Glue is used alongside Amazon Athena to categorize data, clean it, enrich it, and move it between various data stores. AWS Glue Crawlers automatically store the associated metadata in an AWS Glue Data Catalog, which Athena uses to define the schema of the data.

285. Answer: A

Explanation: Amazon Athena is not a managed cluster platform; that description fits Amazon EMR. Athena is a serverless interactive query service with full standard SQL support using Presto, supports DDL using Hive, and is designed for high durability.

286. Answer: B

Explanation: Personally Identifiable Information. PII refers to personal data that can be used to establish an individual's identity and could potentially be exploited in identity theft and financial fraud.

287. Answer: C

Explanation: Amazon Athena can be used to query and analyze AWS cost and usage reports, among other data analysis tasks. It enables businesses to generate insights from their data stored in S3.

288. Answer: B

Explanation: Amazon Macie uses Natural Language Processing methods to help classify different data types and content, making it more effective at identifying sensitive information.

289. Answer: D

Explanation: Amazon Macie uses machine learning to actively review data and user behavior within an AWS account to detect and protect sensitive data.

290. Answer: C

Explanation: Amazon EMR is a managed cluster platform that simplifies running big data frameworks, such as Apache Hadoop and Apache Spark, on AWS to process and analyze large volumes of data.

291. Answer: B

Explanation. Under the AWS shared responsibility model, customers are responsible for managing the security of their operating system, any associated application software, and the configuration of the AWS-provided security group firewall. They must protect the confidentiality, integrity, and availability of their data in the cloud.

292. Answer: B

Explanation: The Cost Optimization check in AWS Trusted Advisor helps to identify idle resources and provides recommendations on how to reduce costs.

293. Answer: B

Explanation: For AWS-managed services such as Amazon RDS or Redshift, AWS manages the configuration work, so customers do not need to worry about it.

294. Answer: C

Explanation: The Payment Card Industry Data Security Standard (PCI DSS) is a security standard for entities that handle online payments using credit cards and store, process, or transmit cardholder data. These entities need to be PCI DSS Level 1 compliant.

295. Answer: B

Explanation: The AWS Acceptable Use Policy encourages or requires users to report any violations of the AUP or suspected security vulnerabilities to AWS.

296. Answer: B

Explanation: ISO 27001 is a security management standard that specifies security management best practices and comprehensive security controls. It is an example of a compliance certification or attestation that AWS undergoes.

297. Answer: C

Explanation: AWS WAF can penetrate layer seven of the OSI model and analyze network traffic at the application layer. It can inspect data and block traffic if it detects threats such as cross-site scripting attacks or SQL injections.

298. Answer: C

Explanation: The AWS Compliance Program is focused on providing certifications/attestations, ensuring compliance with laws, regulations, and privacy, and aligning with security or compliance requirements for specific industries or functions.

299. Answer: C

Explanation: When using IaaS services like Amazon EC2 and VPC, customers are responsible for handling all the security configuration and management tasks themselves.

300. Answer: C

Explanation: G-Cloud [UK] is a framework between the UK government and cloud-based service providers, enabling public bodies to procure commodity-based, pay-as-you-go cloud services on government-approved short-term contracts.

301. Answer: B

Explanation: Amazon Kinesis Video Streams is mainly designed to stream live video from devices to the AWS Cloud, enabling real-time video processing and analytics applications. It offers more than just video data storage, as it allows for real-time viewing of video feeds as they arrive in the cloud and supports various data sources like security cameras and webcams.

302. Answer: D

Explanation: Amazon Kinesis Video Streams can handle a wide range of data types, not just video. It can stream audio, thermal imaging, depth data, RADAR data, and other non-video time-serialized data, making it versatile for different applications.

303. Answer: C

Explanation: Consumers, or Kinesis Video Streams apps, can process video streaming data both in real-time as it's being streamed or after it has been stored, providing flexibility in how they choose to process the incoming data.

304. Answer: B

Explanation: Amazon Kinesis Data Analytics is used for processing and analyzing streaming data using SQL. It allows the development of applications that can perform real-time analytics on data as it streams in from sources like Amazon Kinesis Data Streams and Amazon Kinesis Data Firehose.

305. Answer: B

Explanation: AWS OpenSearch Service is a managed service that facilitates the deployment, operation, and scaling of OpenSearch and Elasticsearch engines. It handles administrative tasks and makes it easier for users to focus on utilizing these engines for their specific needs.

306. Answer: C

Explanation: AWS OpenSearch Service manages various administrative tasks such as hardware provisioning, software installation, setup, monitoring, and backups. This service allows users to concentrate on leveraging the OpenSearch and Elasticsearch engines for their applications.

307. Answer: B

Explanation: AWS OpenSearch Service is commonly used for full-text search, log analytics, real-time application monitoring, and various analytics applications, thanks to its powerful search and indexing capabilities.

308. Answer: B

Explanation: AWS Data Exchange is a service that allows users to discover, subscribe to, and use third-party data in the cloud. It serves as a marketplace for data providers and subscribers to exchange data sets.

309. Answer: B

Explanation: AWS Data Exchange offers encryption and access controls to ensure data security and compliance with regulatory requirements, which includes features like integration with AWS Key Management Service (KMS) for encryption and AWS Identity and Access Management (IAM) for access control.

310. Answer: C

Explanation: AWS OpenSearch Service pricing is based on factors like instance types, storage, data transfer, and additional features like dedicated master nodes or UltraWarm storage. AWS Data Exchange follows a Pay-As-You-Go pricing model, where users pay for the data they consume without any upfront fees.

311. Answer: C

Explanation: HDFS is a scalable, distributed file system designed for Hadoop, which stores data across multiple instances in a cluster. It maintains multiple copies of data on separate instances, ensuring data is not lost if an instance fails. This provides fault tolerance and is essential for reliable data storage and processing in Hadoop-based applications.

312. Answer: B

Explanation: EMRFS (EMR File System) is an enhancement in Amazon EMR that allows it to access data stored in Amazon S3 as if it were a file system like HDFS. This allows clusters to leverage the durability and scalability of S3 for storing input and output data while using HDFS for intermediate results.

313. Answer: C

Explanation: YARN is the default resource manager for Amazon EMR, which handles the management of computational resources in the cluster and the scheduling of user jobs. It is a key component of Apache Hadoop 2.0 and enables the cluster to process various data-processing frameworks.

314. Answer: D

Explanation: SPICE (Super-fast, Parallel, In-memory Calculation Engine) is not a component of AWS Data Pipeline; it is a part of Amazon QuickSight as its in-memory engine. AWS Data Pipeline components include a pipeline definition, which specifies the business logic of your data management, and Task Runner, which searches and completes tasks.

315. Answer: B

Explanation: AWS Data Pipeline is a web service designed to facilitate the automatic movement and transformation of data between AWS compute and storage services, as well as on-premises data sources, at specified intervals. It handles data workflow dependencies and ensures that data is processed as designed.

316. Answer: C

Explanation: Amazon QuickSight is a business intelligence service that enables users to build visualizations, perform ad-hoc analysis, and get business insights from their data. It's designed to be fast and user-friendly, allowing insights to be shared across an organization.

317. Answer: D

Explanation: Amazon EMR primarily supports two processing frameworks: Hadoop MapReduce and Apache Spark. Hadoop MapReduce is a programming model for distributed computing. At the same time, Apache Spark is an open-source distributed processing system that also allows for in-memory caching and processing of large data sets.

318. Answer: B

Explanation: SPICE refers to the Super-fast, Parallel, In-memory Calculation Engine, which is the in-memory processing engine for Amazon QuickSight. It accelerates the performance of analytical queries against imported data and enables quick interaction with visualizations.

319. Answer: B

Explanation: The local file system on each node, which refers to the instance store volumes, is used to store data that is only retained for the lifespan of the Amazon EC2 instance. It is typically used for storing intermediate results during processing tasks within the cluster.

320. Answer: D

Explanation: The Task Runner in AWS Data Pipeline is responsible for polling for tasks and then performing them, such as moving data to Amazon S3 or creating EMR clusters. Task Runner is a key component that helps execute the tasks defined in the pipeline definition.

321. Answer: C

Explanation: Amazon Lex is the AWS service designed for building conversational interfaces for applications using both speech and text. It provides developers with the same conversational engine that powers

Amazon Alexa, allowing for the integration of sophisticated, natural language chatbots into applications.

322. Answer: B

Explanation: Amazon Lex combines the power of Natural Language Understanding (NLU) with Automated Voice Recognition (ASR) to enable developers to create conversational interfaces that can understand user intent and engage in life-like interactions.

323. Answer: B

Explanation: Amazon Polly is the AWS service that converts text into life-like speech. It uses advanced deep-learning technologies to synthesize speech that sounds like a human voice.

324. Answer: A

Explanation: Amazon Comprehend can analyze a document and provide insights such as identifying entities, extracting key phrases, detecting personally identifiable information (PII), determining the main language, identifying sentiment, targeted sentiment, and parsing syntax.

325. Answer: C

Explanation: Amazon Rekognition is designed to provide visual search and image recognition capabilities, allowing developers to integrate these features into their applications.

326. Answer: A

VERSAtile Reads

Explanation: Amazon Lex chatbots transform incoming voice to text and comprehend user intent to provide an intelligent response, enabling natural and engaging conversational experiences.

327. Answer: C

Explanation: With Amazon Polly, you can choose from different languages, select male or female voices, and even specify the accent for the voice to render your speech output.

328. Answer: B

Explanation: Amazon Lex offers built-in integration with several AWS services, including AWS Lambda, Amazon CloudWatch, and Amazon DynamoDB, allowing developers to easily connect their chatbots to serverless business logic and data storage options.

329. Answer: B

Explanation: Amazon Comprehend uses Natural Language Processing (NLP) to extract insights from text, such as identifying entities, key phrases, language, sentiments, and other features.

330. Answer: A

Explanation: Amazon Comprehend is capable of determining the main sentiment expressed in a document, which can be positive, neutral, negative, or mixed emotions.

331. Answer: C

Explanation: Amazon Comprehend is used to analyze and extract insights from documents. It examines texts to detect the dominant language, key phrases, personally identifiable information (PII), sentiment, targeted sentiment, syntax, and topics.

332. Answer: C

Explanation: Real-time database management is not a feature of Amazon Comprehend. Amazon Comprehend features include Detect Key Phrases, Topic Modeling, and Analyze Syntax, among others.

333. Answer: A

Explanation: Amazon Comprehend offers Single-Document Processing, Multiple Document Synchronous Processing, and Asynchronous Batch Processing for analyzing documents.

334. Answer: B

Explanation: Amazon SageMaker assists data scientists and developers by providing an environment to build, train, and deploy machine learning models quickly and efficiently.

335. Answer: A

Explanation: The typical workflow in Amazon SageMaker involves Generating Example Data, Training a Model, and Deploying the Model.

336. Answer: B

Explanation: Amazon Translate provides Neural Machine Translation to translate text across supported languages.

337. Answer: C

Explanation: Amazon Translate costs a fraction (0.05%) of the average cost of human translation, making it a more affordable option.

338. Answer: D

Explanation: AWS Cloud9 is a cloud-based Integrated Development Environment (IDE) that enables code editing and debugging.

339. Answer: B

Explanation: AWS Cloud9 offers built-in features for serverless app developers to create, edit, execute, debug, and deploy AWS Lambda functions directly from the IDE.

340. Answer: B

Explanation: AWS Cloud9 supports collaborative development by allowing developers to access their development environment from any internet-connected device, freeing them from the constraints of a single development workstation.

341. Answer: B

Explanation: Amazon Virtual Private Cloud (Amazon VPC) allows users to provision a logically isolated section of the AWS cloud. Within this isolated environment, users can launch AWS resources in a virtual network that they define, giving them control over their virtual networking environment, including IP address ranges, subnets, and network gateways. This level of isolation and control ensures that resources within a VPC are segregated from those of other users on AWS.

342. Answer: B

Explanation: Multiple connectivity options in an Amazon VPC include connecting directly to the internet using public subnets, connecting to the internet using Network Address Translation for private subnets, creating secure connections to corporate data centers, and connecting privately to other VPCs or AWS services using VPC Endpoints, without using an internet gateway.

343. Answer: C

Explanation: VPC Peering Connection enables EC2 instances in the EC2-Classic platform to communicate with instances in a VPC using private IP addresses. It allows traffic to be routed between two peered VPCs privately without the need for public IP addresses.

344. Answer: C

Explanation: An Internet Gateway serves as the VPC side of a connection to the public internet. It allows resources within the VPC, such as EC2 instances, to access the internet and vice versa, providing a pathway for internet connectivity.

345. Answer: B

Explanation: AWS Lambda is a serverless compute service that allows users to run code without the need to provision or manage servers. It automatically handles the server and infrastructure management tasks, enabling users to run code for applications or backend services with minimal administration.

346. Answer: C

Explanation: AWS Direct Connect provides a dedicated network connection from an organization's premises to AWS. This dedicated connection can lead to reduced network costs, increased bandwidth throughput, and a more consistent network experience compared to internet-based connections.

347. Answer: B

Explanation: An Egress-only Internet Gateway is a stateful gateway used to provide egress-only access for IPv6 traffic from the VPC to the internet. This enables IPv6-enabled resources within a VPC to connect to the internet while preventing the internet from initiating connections with those resources.

348. Answer: C

Explanation: Elastic Load Balancing is not a component of Amazon VPC but rather works with Amazon VPC to provide networking and security features. The components of Amazon VPC include Subnets, Customer Gateways, and VPC Endpoints, among others.

349. Answer: D

Explanation: A NAT Gateway is a highly available, managed Network Address Translation service that allows resources in a private subnet to access the internet while preventing the internet from initiating direct connections with those resources. It is used to enable outbound internet access for instances that do not have public IP addresses.

350. Answer: C

Explanation: Combining a VPN with AWS Direct Connect is beneficial when you need a more reliable and consistent connection to AWS and also requires the traffic to be encrypted. This setup provides the advantages of a dedicated line to AWS through Direct Connect, with the added security of VPN encryption.

351. Answer: C

Explanation: AWS Batch is designed to process large workloads in smaller chunks or batches, especially for longer-running jobs. It dynamically provisions instances based on the volume and allows for the execution of batch computing workloads on the AWS Cloud.

352. Answer: D

Explanation: Amazon CodeCommit is a secure, highly scalable, managed source control service that hosts private Git repositories and is designed to handle everything from code to binaries.

353. Answer: C

Explanation: In AWS Batch, a Job Definition specifies how jobs should be executed, including which Docker container images to use to run the jobs, the required memory and CPU power, and other job-related parameters.

354. Answer: B

Explanation: AWS CodeDeploy is a service that automates code deployments to various instances, including Amazon EC2, AWS Lambda functions, and on-premises instances, helping to facilitate the rapid release of new features and maintain application uptime.

355. Answer: D

Explanation: AWS CodeBuild is a fully managed build service that compiles source code, runs unit tests, and produces deployable artifacts, thereby enabling continuous integration and delivery.

356. Answer: C

Explanation: AWS CodeDeploy helps maintain application uptime by performing in-place updates with rolling deployments, which allows the application to remain available to users while new versions are being deployed.

357. Answer: B

Explanation: Amazon S3 is not a computing platform; it is a storage service. AWS CodeDeploy supports deployments to Amazon EC2, on-premises servers, AWS Lambda, and Amazon ECS.

358. Answer: B

Explanation: AWS CodePipeline is a continuous delivery service that automates the build, test, and release processes, allowing developers to model, visualize, and automate the steps necessary for software deployment.

359. Answer: C

Explanation: In AWS Batch, the Job Queue is responsible for routing submitted jobs to a specific computing environment where the jobs will remain until scheduled to run.

360. Answer: C

Explanation: AWS CodeCommit can be used to store code, binaries, and version-controlled data such as scripts, configurations, HTML pages, and images, making it suitable for a wide range of users in addition to software developers.

361. Answer: C

Explanation: AWS Cloud9 primarily functions as a web-based integrated development environment (IDE) that allows developers to write, run, and debug their code with just a browser.

362. Answer: B

Explanation: AWS Cloud9 can create an EC2 environment by launching an Amazon EC2 instance and connecting your development environment to this newly launched instance

363. Answer: D

Explanation: Amazon Kendra is an AI-powered enterprise search service that enables users to search through vast amounts of content using natural language queries.

364. Answer: B

Explanation: Amazon Textract is a service that automatically extracts text and data from scanned documents, using machine learning to process various document types.

365. Answer: C

Explanation: Amazon Transcribe can analyze live audio streams and provide real-time transcriptions, leveraging automatic speech recognition technology.

366. Answer: B

Explanation: Amazon Rekognition provides highly accurate facial analysis and facial search capabilities, which can be used to detect, analyze, and compare faces for various applications.

367. Answer: C

Explanation: An SSH environment in AWS Cloud9 is created when the platform links an environment to an existing cloud computing instance or your server.

368. Answer: D

Explanation: The solution proposed for Cleveland Medical Center involves using Amazon Rekognition's facial analysis feature to identify patients, which requires uploading pictures of patients at the time of making an appointment.

369. Answer: C

Explanation: A "Cloud First" strategy emphasizes using cloud services to provide scalability to meet demands and to pay only for utilized resources, reducing the need for investment in and maintenance of on-premises IT resources.

370. Answer: C

Explanation: By saving the environment in the cloud, AWS Cloud9 allows developers to easily switch between different computers and enables faster onboarding of new team members without being tied to a single machine or server setup.

371. Answer: C

Explanation: AWS Lambda represents serverless architecture, where there are no servers to manage, and it allows code execution in response to events without provisioning or managing infrastructure.

372. Answer: C

Explanation: API Gateway is used to make API calls that trigger Lambda functions, as opposed to traditional architectures where a load balancer would serve a similar purpose.

373. Answer: D

Explanation: In a truly serverless architecture, DynamoDB is often used for storage as it integrates well with AWS Lambda and allows you to pay only for the storage and throughput you use.

374. Answer: B

Explanation: AWS Lambda offers the first 1 million requests for free and, after that, charges $0.20 per 1 million requests.

375. Answer: A

Explanation: The duration cost of AWS Lambda is $0.00001667 for every GB-second used, rounded up to the nearest 100 milliseconds.

376. Answer: A

Explanation: Ruby is not listed as a supported language for AWS Lambda. AWS Lambda currently supports Node.js, Java, Python, C#, Go, and PowerShell.

377. Answer: B

Explanation: AWS Lambda supports version control, allowing you to have multiple versions of your code and the ability to roll back to previous versions if necessary.

378. Answer: C

Explanation: Amazon is responsible for the hardware, operating systems, security patching, antivirus, and the physical security of data centers, among other things, under the shared responsibility model.

379. Answer: C

Explanation: AWS Lambda automatically scales out, meaning it runs code in response to each event individually, which can result in concurrent execution as needed.

380. Answer: B

Explanation: With AWS Lambda's cost-optimized pricing, you only pay for the actual computing time consumed, measured in milliseconds, when your code is running. There are no charges when your code is not running.

381. Answer: B

Explanation: An AWS Fargate task definition is a text file in JSON format that can describe a maximum of ten containers. This serves as the blueprint for the application, defining various parameters such as operating system parameters, containers used, ports, and data volumes.

382. Answer: B

Explanation: Amazon ECS clusters serve as a logical grouping of tasks or services and can be used to isolate your applications. When tasks are run on Fargate, AWS Fargate manages the cluster resources on your behalf.

383. Answer: D

Explanation: AWS Fargate eliminates the need to provision, configure, and scale virtual machine clusters to run containers, which means you do not have to worry about selecting server types, scaling clusters, or optimizing cluster packing.

384. Answer: C

Explanation: Amazon Lightsail provides everything you need to get your project up and running, including virtual machines, containers, databases, CDN, load balancers, DNS management, and a low, predictable monthly fee.

385. Answer: B

Explanation: AWS Outposts allows you to run cloud services in your internal data center, supporting workloads that must remain on-premises due to latency or data sovereignty needs, thus providing a hybrid deployment model.

386. Answer: C

VERSAtile Reads

Explanation: Amazon Lightsail is designed for developers, small businesses, students, and other users who require a simple solution for building and hosting cloud-based applications. It is best suited for small projects that need quick deployments.

387. Answer: C

Explanation: AWS Fargate is considered serverless and is used to manage containers without the need to manage servers or clusters of Amazon EC2 instances.

388. Answer: C

Explanation: AWS Outposts is designed to function with a constant and continuous connection between your Outpost and an AWS Region. You must connect your Outpost to your on-premises network and the region for it to function properly.

389. Answer: C

Explanation: An Outpost subnet can extend any VPC in the region to your Outpost, effectively expanding the VPC's reach to include the on-premises location where the Outpost is deployed.

390. Answer: B

Explanation: For EC2 instances operating in Outposts subnets, the Amazon Route 53 DNS Service is used to resolve domain names to IP addresses for network interfaces connected to a VPC. Route 53 provides DNS functionality, including domain registration, DNS routing, and health checks.

391. Answer: A

Explanation: AWS CodePipeline is a continuous delivery service designed to automate the development, testing, and production deployment of applications. It streamlines the release process by managing the workflow from source code to deployment.

392. Answer: D

Explanation: AWS X-Ray helps developers debug and analyze their production applications by providing a map of application components and the request flow end to end, which includes tracing calls to databases and other resources.

393. Answer: B

Explanation: A stage in AWS CodePipeline is a logical unit that may include different actions like building, testing, or deploying code. Stages help organize the release process into distinct steps.

394. Answer B

Explanation: AWS CodeStar is designed to enable collaborative work on development projects, providing an integrated dashboard for managing the entire development pipeline and integrating with services like CodeCommit, CodeBuild, and CodeDeploy.

395. Answer: C

Explanation: In AWS CodePipeline, an 'action' refers to an operation that is performed on the application code at a certain stage of the pipeline. These actions are the fundamental building blocks of a pipeline and are defined within stages.

VERSAtile Reads

396. Answer: C

Explanation: A pipeline execution can be manually stopped, which puts it in a "Stopping" state until it is fully stopped. There are two ways to stop an execution: "Stop and wait" and "Stop and abandon."

397. Answer: B

Explanation: Amazon CodeArtifact is a package management service that allows developers to securely store, publish, and share software packages, supporting multiple package formats and integrating with other AWS services.

398. Answer: C

Explanation: A pipeline in AWS CodePipeline defines the process of releasing software updates, which includes a series of stages and actions that manage the flow from source code to deployment.

399. Answer: C

Explanation: AWS CodeStar includes a centralized project dashboard that provides a high-level overview of project activities, a toolchain, and the ability to manage access, monitor, and collaborate on projects from a single location.

400. Answer: C

Explanation: A source revision in AWS CodePipeline is a specific version of a source change, such as a commit in a repository, that causes the pipeline to execute. It processes only that source revision during an execution.

401. Answer: C

Explanation: AWS Direct Connect is designed to establish a dedicated, logical network connection from a customer's remote network to AWS. This service enables a private link between the customer's data center or co-location environment and AWS, which helps reduce network costs, increase bandwidth throughput, and provide a more consistent network experience than internet-based connections.

402. Answer: A

Explanation: AWS Direct Connect offers significant benefits such as cost reduction and increased reliability. By transferring data to and from AWS directly, it reduces network costs for high bandwidth workloads and charges data transfer at reduced rates. It also provides a consistent network experience with reduced network latency compared to internet connections.

403. Answer: B

Explanation: AWS Direct Connect allows for both public and private connections. Public VIFs enable access to AWS services such as Amazon S3 and EC2 instances using public IP addresses. It bypasses the public internet, providing a direct and private connection to AWS.

404. Answer: B

Explanation: AWS Direct Connect uses a fiber optic cable to link the customer's internal network to an AWS Direct Connect location. This dedicated connection runs from the customer's router to an AWS Direct Connect router, bypassing ISPs and providing a private and direct connection to AWS.

405. Answer: B

Explanation: When using AWS Direct Connect with private virtual interfaces (VIFs), data transfer into an AWS account is free. This means that inbound traffic does not incur additional charges, which can lead to cost savings, especially for high-volume data ingress scenarios.

406. Answer: A

Explanation: The network zone in AWS Global Accelerator is responsible for providing a set of Static IP addresses from the AWS edge network. These addresses act as a single fixed entry point for client connections to the Global Accelerator.

407. Answer: C

Explanation: The traffic dial within AWS Global Accelerator allows you to control the percentage of traffic that is directed to an endpoint group. By adjusting the traffic dial setting, you can test new AWS releases or conduct blue/green deployment tests with varying amounts of traffic.

408. Answer: C

Explanation: In AWS Global Accelerator, an endpoint serves as the destination for traffic that has been routed through the accelerator. Endpoints can be Application Load Balancers, Network Load Balancers, Elastic IP addresses, or EC2 instances. They receive traffic based on factors such as geo-proximity, health, and configured weights.

409. Answer: D

Explanation: AWS Direct Connect allows for a private VIF (virtual interface) based connection to Amazon VPC, which enables a private and direct connection without going through the internet. This ensures a secure, stable, and consistent connection to the VPC.

410. Answer: C

Explanation: The primary difference between AWS Direct Connect and a VPN Connection is that Direct Connect uses a dedicated, private connection from your network to AWS, bypassing the public internet. In contrast, a VPN Connection creates a secure, encrypted tunnel over the internet to connect two networks. Direct Connect provides a more reliable and consistent network experience with potentially higher throughput and lower latency.

411. Answer: C

Explanation: IT assets were changed from programmable to provisioned resources in October 2018. This means that IT assets, which were previously programmable resources, are now available as provisioned resources, allowing for more flexibility and scalability within the cloud environment.

412. Answer: B

Explanation: Cloud scalability refers to how well a framework can respond and adjust to evolving requests, ensuring the system can handle growth by adding resources without losing quality of service or experiencing interruptions, as well as efficiently downscaling when necessary.

413. Answer: C

Explanation: AWS CloudFormation is the service that allows users to manage their AWS infrastructure using templates written in JSON. With CloudFormation, resources like EC2 instances, RDS instances, and S3 buckets can be created and managed as code.

414. Answer: C

Explanation: A golden image is a snapshot of a particular state of a resource. It allows for faster start times when launching instances since it removes dependencies on configuration services or third-party repositories by providing a pre-configured state.

415. Answer: B

Explanation: AWS CloudWatch Alarms can monitor AWS resources and applications, sending an Amazon SNS message when a particular metric exceeds a specified threshold for a predetermined number of periods, enabling proactive responses to system events.

416. Answer: B

Explanation: Amazon Route 53 is a service used to register and manage domain names. It is a scalable Domain Name System (DNS) web service and is global, not tied to any particular AWS region.

417. Answer: B

Explanation: A stateless application does not need knowledge of previous interactions and does not store session information. An example of a stateless application is AWS Lambda, which processes requests without needing to remember past interactions.

418. Answer: C

Explanation: AWS Lambda provides a serverless architecture, meaning that users do not need to manage the underlying infrastructure. It executes code in response to events and automatically manages the compute resources.

419. Answer: C

VERSAtile Reads

Explanation: In AWS, systems can be scaled in two ways: Scale Up, which involves increasing the specifications of an individual resource, and scale out, which means increasing the number of resources to distribute the workload.

420. Answer: C

Explanation: AWS-managed services offer building blocks that developers can use to power their applications, helping organizations to move faster and lower IT costs. They eliminate the need to manage the underlying infrastructure, allowing teams to focus on developing their applications.

421. Answer: B

Explanation: AWS Application Discovery Service is designed to help plan migration projects to the AWS Cloud by gathering information about on-premises data centers. It collects usage and configuration data from servers to assist in the planning of migrations, making option B the correct answer. The other options are not the primary purposes of this service.

422. Answer: B

Explanation: Amazon S3 is famous for its scalability and resilience, as it adjusts automatically to varying storage needs without downtime.

423. Answer: C

Explanation: The AWS Agentless Discovery Connector is used to perform agentless discovery when deployed through VMware vCenter, identifying VMs and hosts.

424. Answer: A

Explanation: Amazon Redshift Serverless automatically scales compute clusters based on workload predictions to optimize cost and performance.

425. Answer: B

Explanation: Amazon One Enterprise uses palm scanning technology, which combines palm and vein imagery for highly accurate and contactless identity verification.

426. Answer: C

Explanation: Amazon Q in QuickSight uses generative AI to transform data into narratives and insights, which makes it a generative BI capabilities feature.

427. Answer: A

Explanation: AWS Transit Gateway Connect is designed to simplify connecting on-premises networks to Amazon VPCs and Transit Gateways, offering improved routing and management capabilities.

428. Answer: A

Explanation: Amazon ElastiCache Serverless eliminates the need for capacity planning and manual patching. This service focuses on simplifying data management.

429. Answer: B

Explanation: Amazon Q, in its Generative AI Assistant form, acts as a digital assistant, helping employees with tasks such as answering questions and generating content.

430. Answer: D

Explanation: Amazon EBS Snapshots on Amazon S3 Glacier Deep Archive provides long-term storage for EBS snapshots at an incredibly low cost.

431. Answer: C

Explanation: AWS's "Pay as you go" pricing policy means that you only pay for the exact amount of computing resources you consume, with no need for upfront capital investment or fixed monthly fees. This approach ensures that you only incur charges based on your actual usage of AWS services, allowing for flexible and cost-effective scaling.

432. Answer: A

Explanation: The "Pay less when you reserve" pricing model allows you to reserve capacity in advance, providing significant savings of up to 60% compared to the equivalent On-demand capacity. This is ideal for predictable workloads where long-term planning is possible.

433. Answer: B

Explanation: The AWS Price List Query API is designed to retrieve specific pricing information, such as the cost of Amazon EC2 instances in a particular region. Unlike the Bulk API, the Query API is suitable for retrieving targeted pricing details for specific AWS services and products.

434. Answer: A

Explanation: AWS Free Tier offers new customers the opportunity to try out AWS services for free, giving them hands-on experience with the platform. Some services within the Free Tier are available at no charge for the first 12 months, while others remain free indefinitely.

435. Answer: A

Explanation: AWS Elastic Beanstalk is a service that allows you to deploy and manage applications in the AWS cloud without any charge for the service itself. However, the resources that it provisions, such as EC2 instances or RDS instances, are not free of charge and will incur costs based on usage.

436. Answer: A

Explanation: When using AWS, the three fundamental characteristics that influence costs are Compute, Storage, and Data Transfer Out. These core characteristics vary depending on the AWS product but generally determine the overall cost incurred for using AWS services.

437. Answer: B

Explanation: Reserved Instances offer the option to reserve compute capacity for a 1 or 3-year term, providing significant discounts compared to On-Demand Instance pricing. Customers can opt for no upfront payment or make a low one-time upfront payment to further reduce hourly costs.

438. Answer: B

Explanation: AWS Cost Explorer is a tool that provides an interface for visualizing, understanding, and managing AWS costs and usage over time. It is used to explore and analyze costs that have already been incurred.

439. Answer: C

Explanation: Consolidated Billing in AWS allows you to combine the billing for multiple AWS accounts into one account. This helps in obtaining volume-based discounts (tiering benefits) by aggregating usage across all linked accounts.

440. Answer: C

Explanation: While storage class, the number and size of objects stored, and the amount of data transferred out do affect the cost of Amazon S3, the geographic region of your bucket does not directly affect the cost. AWS S3 pricing is generally consistent across regions, but data transfer and operational request costs can vary by region.

441. Answer: C

Explanation: Each resource can have a maximum of 50 user-created tags. System-created tags that begin with AWS are reserved for AWS use and do not count against this limit.

442. Answer: D

Explanation: You can add tags to an AWS resource when you create it, and you can also add, change, or remove tags any time after the resource has been created.

443. Answer: C

Explanation: Tag Editor allows you to add tags to multiple resources at once, search for resources, and manage tags across services and regions.

444. Answer: C

Explanation: You can edit tag keys and values and remove tags from a resource at any time.

445. Answer: D

Explanation: When you delete a resource in AWS, associated tags are also automatically deleted to maintain consistency, simplify management, avoid confusion, and promote efficiency in resource tagging.

446. Answer: C

Explanation: Tags function like resource properties, meaning they are shared across the entire AWS account.

447. Answer: B

Explanation: Tagging AWS resources helps organize them and simplifies resource and access management as well as cost allocation.

448. Answer: C

Explanation: By listing resources with specific tags, you can execute management tasks at scale, like deleting or terminating resources.

449. Answer: B

Explanation: Tagging can be used to automate the shutdown or removal of a set of resources at the end of the working day.

450. Answer: B

Explanation: Creating and implementing an AWS tagging standard across your organization's accounts will enable you to manage and govern your AWS environments consistently.

451. Answer: C

Explanation: The paying master account in AWS Organizations is primarily used for consolidated billing purposes. It is the single AWS account that serves as the paying account for all other interconnected AWS accounts within the organization, providing a combined view of charges and generating an expense report for each participant account.

452. Answer: C

Explanation: One of the significant advantages of using consolidated billing is the ability to combine usage across all accounts to share volume pricing discounts and saving plans. This can result in cost savings as the organization benefits from lower-tiered pricing due to aggregated usage.

453. Answer: C

Explanation: The paying account should only be used for billing purposes and not for deploying resources. By focusing the paying account on billing, organizations can avoid the complexity and potential security risks associated with deploying resources in the billing account.

454. Answer: C

Explanation: There is a soft limit of 20 accounts per AWS Organization. This means that typically, you can have up to 20 accounts within a single organization, although this limit can be increased upon request to AWS Support.

455. Answer: B

Explanation: With consolidated billing, AWS determines the pricing tier to apply for volume discounts by combining the usage from all accounts within the organization. This aggregated usage can lead to lower costs as it allows the organization to reach higher discount tiers.

456. Answer: D

Explanation: When consolidated billing is enabled, unused Reserved Instances for EC2 are applied across the group. This means that if any account within the organization purchases Reserved Instances, the cost-benefit can be shared among all the accounts in the organization.

457. Answer: B

Explanation: AWS Billing Conductor is a customizable billing service that allows organizations to align their billing data with their intended chargeback or showback business logic. It provides the ability to distribute credits and fees, share overhead costs, and customize billing rates for different accounts.

458. Answer: B

Explanation: Billing groups in AWS Billing Conductor provide a contextual understanding of consumption and costs by grouping accounts with similar financial owners. This helps in gaining cross-account billing visibility and managing the costs effectively.

459. Answer: C

Explanation: AWS Billing Conductor's rate management feature allows organizations to build pricing rules that can be global, billing entity, service, or SKU-specific. These rules can be combined to set the rate that end users will see in the billing interface and Cost & Usage Report (CUR).

460. Answer: B

Explanation: In AWS Billing Conductor, commitment-based discounts like Savings Plans and Reserved Instance purchases are contextual to the billing group. If an account purchases such discounts within the billing group, the entire group can benefit. However, accounts outside the billing group do not benefit from these discounts.

461. Answer: B

Explanation: The AWS Knowledge Center is designed to help customers stay informed about the latest changes in the AWS environment, troubleshoot issues, and find answers to their questions.

462. Answer: A

Explanation: The AWS Knowledge Center provides detailed documentation on AWS services, best practices, and use cases, helping users understand and proficiently implement AWS services.

463. Answer: B

Explanation: Community members can typically contribute user-generated insights, advice, and solutions. This content adds value by sharing experiences, knowledge, and solutions to common problems within the community. It fosters collaboration, discussion, and learning among community members.

464. Answer: A

Explanation: The Knowledge Center offers video resources such as webinars, tutorials, and interviews to share knowledge and best practices in a multimedia format.

465. Answer: B

Explanation: The Knowledge Center provides topic-based navigation, which allows users to easily explore specific areas of interest.

466. Answer: C

Explanation: AWS Professional Services helps customers in migrating their on-premises applications to the cloud, among other cloud-based initiatives.

467. Answer: B

Explanation: AWS Professional Services' vision is centered on customer focus and leveraging AWS for innovative outcomes.

468. Answer: C

Explanation: AWS Professional Services employs a proprietary methodology derived from Amazon's own best practices to help clients achieve project outcomes efficiently.

VERSAtile Reads

469. Answer: B

Explanation: Resource Groups in AWS allow users to create and manage a collection of resources that share one or more tags, facilitating easier management and automation.

470. Answer: B

Explanation: Resource Groups can display a variety of information, including metrics, alarms, and configuration details for the resources within the group.

471. Answer: D

Explanation: The Enterprise Support Plan is the only plan among the options listed that includes a Technical Account Manager (TAM). This plan is designed for highly complex environments and customers who need a dedicated person for customer service and proactive management.

.

472. Answer: C

Explanation: For a Production System Down case, where business functions are significantly impacted and important functions of the application are unavailable, the Business Support Plan offers a response time of 1 hour

473. Answer: C

Explanation: On-Site Support is a feature exclusive to the Enterprise Support Plan. While both Enterprise and Enterprise On-Ramp plans offer advanced troubleshooting and infrastructure event management, On-Site Support is not provided with the Enterprise On-Ramp Plan.

474. Answer: B

Explanation: The Developer Support Plan is available at a cost of $29 per month. It is designed to support customers in the early stages of development or testing on AWS.

475. Answer: A

Explanation: The Basic Support Plan is ideal for individuals and small businesses just starting with AWS. It is a free plan that offers support for account and billing queries, service limit increases, access to support forums, and AWS documentation.

476. Answer: B

Explanation: The Developer Support Plan guides using AWS products, features, and services for non-production workloads. It is tailored for customers who are in the testing or early development phase.

477. Answer: D

Explanation: The Enterprise Support Plan offers a response time of less than 15 minutes for a Business-Critical System Down case. This level of service is for situations where critical application functions are unavailable, and the business is at risk.

478. Answer: B

Explanation: The AWS Trusted Advisor inspects user environments and provides recommendations for best practices and optimization. It helps in identifying cost-saving opportunities, closing security gaps, and optimizing the infrastructure.

479. Answer: C

Explanation: The Business Support Plan is recommended for customers who run applications in production environments and rely on their solutions to be available, scalable, and secured. It is suitable for customers who have multiple services activated or use key services extensively.

480. Answer: C

Explanation: The Enterprise On-Ramp Support Plan offers proactive alerts and a dedicated account manager, among other features. It is ideal for large enterprises with mission-critical workloads and advanced troubleshooting needs.

481. Answer: B

Explanation: The AWS Partner Network (APN) is a global community of partners who build, market, and sell customer offerings by leveraging AWS software, expertise, and resources

482. Answer: B

Explanation: Within the AWS Partner Network (APN), partners are categorized into APN Consulting Partners, like system integrators and managed service providers, and APN Technology Partners, like independent software vendors

483. Answer: B

Explanation: AWS partners can advance to higher performance tiers by meeting certain criteria, including customer engagement, training, and monetary investment and fee thresholds.

484. Answer: C

Explanation: APN Consulting Partners can choose from four performance tiers offered by AWS: Registered, Standard, Advanced, and Premier

485. Answer: B

Explanation: AWS Test Drive is a free program that allows an AWS partner to launch preconfigured server-based tools and workloads in a test environment, accompanied by step-by-step manuals and labs

486. Answer: C

Explanation: The AWS Command Line Interface (AWS CLI) is a unified tool that allows you to manage your AWS services from the command line and automate them through scripts

487. Answer: B

Explanation: SDKs benefit developers by offering pre-built components and libraries, which significantly reduce the time and resources needed for development.

488. Answer: C

Explanation: An API (Application Programming Interface) is a set of programming instructions that allows applications to access and share data, typically through a sequence of requests and responses

489. Answer: C

Explanation: SDKs (Software Development Kits) are used during application development to provide developers with pre-built modules, components, tools, and libraries.

490. Answer: B

Explanation: Game development SDKs typically include sample code, tutorials, 3D graphics libraries, audio libraries, physics engines, artificial intelligence libraries, networking libraries, and development tools, but not physical server hardware

491. Answer: C

Explanation: The AWS SDK is a set of tools and libraries that simplifies the integration of AWS services into applications, allowing developers to work with AWS resources consistently and effectively across various programming languages.

492. Answer: B

Explanation: AWS Config offers continuous monitoring and recording of AWS resource configurations, which aids in auditing, compliance checks, and change tracking.

493. Answer: D

Explanation: AWS OpsWorks is a configuration management service provided by Amazon Web Services (AWS) that helps you automate the management of servers and applications.

494. Answer: C

Explanation: AWS Marketplace is a curated digital catalog where users can find, buy, deploy, and manage third-party software, data, and services to build solutions and run businesses.

495. Answer: B

Explanation: AWS Marketplace offers flexible pricing options, including a free trial, hourly, monthly, annual, multi-year, and Bring Your License (BYOL) models

496. Answer: B

Explanation: Anyone with an AWS account can use AWS Marketplace as a buyer without any additional requirements. It offers a wide range of software and services with flexible payment options and unified billing.

497. Answer: A

Explanation: AWS CloudFormation manages your infrastructure as code, allowing you to define and provision resources in a declarative way.

498. Answer: C

Explanation: AWS Service Catalog helps in standardizing and governing the provisioning of cloud resources, ensuring adherence to security and compliance policies.

499. Answer: A

Explanation:
It is important to ensure that the SDK is from reputable sources, free of dangerous or malicious code, and regularly updated to maintain security.

500. Answer: B

Explanation: The SDK's license agreement is crucial as it must cover all required usage, comply with the law, and not impose any restrictions on the usage or distribution of the apps created with it.

About Our Products

Other products from VERSAtile Reads are:

Elevate Your Leadership: The 10 Must-Have Skills

Elevate Your Leadership: 8 Effective Communication Skills

Elevate Your Leadership: 10 Leadership Styles for Every Situation

300+ PMP Practice Questions Aligned with PMBOK 7, Agile Methods, and Key Process Groups – 2024

Exam-Cram Essentials Last-Minute Guide to Ace the PMP Exam - Your Express Guide featuring PMBOK® Guide

Career Mastery Blueprint - Strategies for Success in Work and Business

Memory Magic: Unraveling the Secret of Mind Mastery

The Success Equation Psychological Foundations For Accomplishment

Fairy Dust Chronicles – The Short and Sweet of Wonder

B2B Breakthrough – Proven Strategies from Real-World Case Studies

VERSAtile Reads

CISSP Fast Track: Master CISSP Essentials for Exam Success

CISA Fast Track: Master CISA Essentials for Exam Success

CISM Fast Track: Master CISM Essentials for Exam Success

CCSP Fast Track: Master CCSP Essentials for Exam Success

Certified SCRUM Master Exam Cram Essentials

AZ-900 Essentials: Fast Track to Exam Success

CISSP Fast Track Master: CISSP Essentials for Exam Success

CISA Fast Track Master: CISA Essentials for Exam Success

CISM Fast Track Master: CISM Essentials for Exam Success

CCSP Fast Track Master: CCSP Essentials for Exam Success

Printed in Great Britain
by Amazon